Other books by Georgia Heard

For the Good of the Earth and Sun

Writing Toward Home

Awakening the Heart

The Revision Toolbox

Climb Inside a Poem (with Lester Laminack)

A Place for Wonder: Reading and Writing Nonfiction in the Primary Grades

Poetry Lessons to Meet the Common Core State Standards

Children's books

Creatures of Earth, Sea, and Sky: Animal Poems

Songs of Myself: An Anthology of Poems and Art

This Place I Know: Poems of Comfort

Falling Down the Page: A Book of List Poems

The Arrow Finds Its Mark: A Book of Found Poems

GEORGIA HEARD

FINDING THE HEART
OF NONFICTION

TEACHING 7 ESSENTIAL CRAFT TOOLS
WITH MENTOR TEXTS

HEINEMANN
Portsmouth, NH

Heinemann
361 Hanover Street
Portsmouth, NH 03801–3912
www.heinemann.com

Offices and agents throughout the world

The author and publisher wish to thank those who have generously given permission to reprint borrowed material:

Excerpts from *Sea Horse: The Shyest Fish in the Sea* by Christine Butterworth. Text copyright © 2006 by Christine Butterworth. Illustrations copyright © 2006 by John Lawrence. Reprinted by permission of Candlewick Press, Somerville, MA, on behalf of Walker Books Ltd., London.

Excerpt from blog entry "Nonfiction: An Update" by Franki Sibberson posted January 9, 2013 on *A Year of Reading*: http://readingyear.blogspot.com/2013/01/nonfiction-update.html. Reprinted by permission of the author.

Acknowledgments for borrowed material continue on page x.

Library of Congress Cataloging-in-Publication Data
Heard, Georgia.
   Finding the heart of nonfiction : teaching 7 essential craft tools with mentor texts / Georgia Heard.
      pages   cm
   Includes bibliographical references.
   ISBN 978-0-325-04647-1
   1. English language—Composition and exercises—Study and teaching. 2. Exposition (Rhetoric)—Study and teaching. 3. Mentoring in education.   I. Title.

LB1576.D635 2009
372.6—dc23   2013018840

Editor: Zoë Ryder White
Production: Vicki Kasabian
Cover and interior designs: Monica Ann Crigler
Typesetter: Kim Arney
Manufacturing: Steve Bernier

Printed in the United States of America on acid-free paper
17   16   15   14   13   EBM   1   2   3   4   5

To Leo—

who inspires me to explore

the world with my heart

Contents

Acknowledgments   xi

Introduction   Mentor Texts: Opening the World to Writing   xiii

PART 1   NONFICTION MENTOR TEXTS: LEARNING TO WRITE FROM WRITERS   1

What Are Mentor Texts?   3

My Nonfiction Mentor Texts   5

Types of Nonfiction   8

Expository Writing   9

Narrative Nonfiction   9

Persuasive, Opinion, and Argumentative Writing   10

Descriptive Nonfiction   11

Choosing Nonfiction Mentor Texts   13

   Try This Modeling with Your Own Mentor Texts   15

   Reproducible My Mentor Text Note-Taking Sheet   19

Reading Nonfiction with Different Lenses   20

   Try This Using Different Lenses to Read   22

Ways to Include Nonfiction Mentor Texts in the Classroom   25

Read-Aloud and Immersion   25

Student Nonfiction Anthologies   27

   Try This Creating Nonfiction Mentor Text Anthologies   28

   Try This Fitting It All in with Nonfiction Mondays   30

Mining Mentor Texts for Craft Teaching Possibilities   33

Keep It Simple   39

1. Focus: The Hearth of Nonfiction Writing   41

Ask Questions   43

Focus on Your Interests and Passion   43

Find Your Purpose and Audience   43

Study Mentor Texts   44

Distill Information   44

    Try This Distilling Information into a Six-Word Memoir   45

    Try This Studying Titles to Learn About Focus   47

    Try This Writing a Poem to Help Focus a Topic   49

2. Turning Facts into Scenes: Writing with Imagery   51

    Try This Writing with Imagery (more experienced writers)   52

    Try This Writing with Imagery (less experienced writers)   55

    Try This Writing Photo-Essays: Being Inspired by Visual Imagery   57

    Reproducible Turning Facts into Scenes: Writing with Imagery   59

3. Leads: The Doorway into Writing   60

Types of Leads   61

    Try This Learning from Leads   64

    Reproducible Leads   66

4. Point of View and Voice: Who Are We When We Write?   68

Point of View   68

    Try This Studying Point of View   70

    Reproducible Point of View   71

Voice: Who Are We When We Write?   73

    Try This Considering Voice   74

    Reproducible Voice: Who Are We When We Write?   75

5. Precise Language: Details, Details, and More Details   76

Sensory Words   77

   Try This   Using Sensory Words   78

   Reproducible   Sensory Words   79

Precise Language: Concrete Nouns and Active Verbs   80

   Try This   Using Precise Language   83

   Reproducible   Precise Language: Concrete Nouns and Active Verbs   84

Figurative Language   85

   Try This   Using Personification to Make Nonfiction Writing Come Alive   88

   Reproducible   Figurative Language: Simile and Metaphor   89

   Reproducible   Figurative Language: Personification   90

Domain-Specific Vocabulary   91

   Try This   Generating Domain-Specific Vocabulary   94

6. Text Structures: Writing Bird by Bird   95

Types of Nonfiction Text Structures   95

Chapters and Sections: Breaking Writing into Parts   98

   Try This   Structuring and Organizing Nonfiction   102

7. Endings: Letting Words Linger   103

Types of Endings   104

   Reproducible   Endings   107

Nuts and Bolts: More Tools of the Nonfiction Trade   108

Using Nonfiction Text Features in Meaningful Ways   108

Using Dialogue and Quotes from Primary Source Material   112

Ensuring Truth and Accuracy   115

Varying Sentence Length   115

Citing Sources and Creating a Bibliography   120

Conclusion   123

Works Cited and Bibliography   125

ACKNOWLEDGMENTS

I am very grateful to the many mentors who surround me and inspire me to do my best. As John C. Crosby wrote, "Mentoring is a brain to pick, an ear to listen, and a push in the right direction." Thank you to my teaching and writing community for listening and pushing me in the right direction. I particularly want to thank the following:

Zoë Ryder White, my wonderful and wise editor, for being the voice of encouragement and enthusiasm throughout the writing of this book. And thanks to team Heinemann for your continuing support of my work and writing over the past twenty years—particularly Patty Adams; Vicki Boyd; Eric Chalek; Monica Ann Crigler; Lisa Fowler; Vicki Kasabian; Anthony Marvullo; Kate Montgomery; Lesa Scott; and Beth Tripp.

The Benjamin School, especially Kristine Ackerman for her brilliant teaching and radiant third-grade classroom where kids are joyfully immersed in studying the world through nonfiction, and Jen McDonough for her extraordinary teaching—and for showing me new ways to help first graders see the world with wonder.

The American Embassy School in New Delhi, India, where I spent an amazing week in conversation and in classrooms with the incredible middle school English and social studies teachers and students—especially Anna Citrino, fellow poet.

Bruce Ballard and the Bronx Charter School for Better Learning for the brilliant idea and samples of six-word memoirs.

My colleagues who have inspired and taught me so much about nonfiction writing over the years, especially Nancie Atwell; Karen Caine; Lucy Calkins; Lynn R. Dorfman and Rose Cappelli; Ralph Fletcher and Joann Portalupi; Stephanie Harvey; Linda Hoyt; Peter Lourie; Laura Robb; and Tony Stead.

My community of friends, who always provide an ear to listen—especially Rebecca Kai Dotlich, Marie Howe, Patricia McNaught, Brigid Collins, and Susan Kimball.

And my family, my husband Dermot and my son Leo, who always support me, especially on bleary-eyed mornings after all-night writing sessions.

INTRODUCTION

Mentor Texts

Opening the World to Writing

Because for some of us, books are as important as almost anything else on earth. What a miracle it is that out of these small, flat, rigid squares of paper unfolds world after world after world, worlds that sing to you, comfort and quiet or excite you. Books help us understand who we are and how we are to behave. They show us what community and friendship mean; they show us how to live and die. They are full of all the things that you don't get in real life—wonderful, lyrical language, for instance, right off the bat. And quality of attention: we may notice amazing details during the course of a day but we rarely let ourselves stop and really pay attention. An author makes you notice, makes you pay attention, and this is a great gift. My gratitude for good writing is unbounded; I'm grateful for it the way I'm grateful for the ocean.

—Anne Lamott, *Bird by Bird*

On my desk is a stack of books. Some people call them mentor texts; I call them guardian angels. These are the books that guide me with a whisper of words, inspiring me to find my own voice as I write. They give me the knowledge and wisdom of what good-quality writing sounds and feels like.

Each day, as I prepare to write I begin by opening a book that I admire, usually in the same genre as I'm writing in. The words coax my own voice to speak. I plumb the books for craft ideas: How is the book organized? What point of view has the author chosen? How does the book begin? How did this author go about researching? Many of my own craft decisions are made as a result of time spent with my mentor texts. They are my teachers of craft, but they also help me realize writing possibilities beyond my own imagination. I let the words pour over me like water on a parched plant and open the world of writing.

Mentor texts are more than just craft coaches for writers—they can also offer inspiration and life lessons. My son went to a sleep-away summer camp when he was eight years old. He was excited to experience camp life. Unfortunately, it was cold and rainy every day, and camp was not what he had expected. He had carried along the book *Hatchet*, by Gary Paulsen (2007). When we picked him up from camp, he was so relieved to see us, and as he was packing up I noticed his tattered and dog-eared copy of *Hatchet* among his belongings. When I asked him about the book, he said, "Mom, *Hatchet* saved me. I knew that if Brian could survive in the Canadian wilderness, I could survive here for three weeks." A bit dramatic but wise for an eight-year-old away from home for the first time. *Hatchet* gave my son resilience and courage, and helped him get through his three-week camp experience. As Anne Lamott writes, "They [books] show us how to live and die" (1994, 15). Or in my son's case, how to survive his first sleep-away camp experience.

As I have worked with students on writing, I've noticed that unless they read, study, and absorb the genre of writing they're writing in, it is difficult for them to write and revise and do the kind of rigorous crafting work that is required of writers.

Most disciplines expect that novices learn from experts, whether they're beginner tennis players watching professional tennis players or art students copying master paintings. Similarly, writers learn by emulation.

Years ago when I took a painting class, my professor asked us to copy master paintings. I grumbled about it, but once I began the arduous process of copying, I discovered things about the composition, color, and even the way the artists applied the brushstrokes that I never saw as an onlooker. The paintings were my teachers in learning how to paint.

When I was a young writing student at Columbia University, my mentor was the poet Stanley Kunitz. I admired his work but he also gave me wise advice about writing. In my early twenties, life in New York City seemed chaotic and overwhelming at times; for comfort I would ride the bus to the Metropolitan Museum of Art, notebook in hand, and stand in front of Renoir's paintings such as *A Girl with a Watering Can* and write poems. Several months into the semester, Stanley Kunitz asked each student to gather a collection of poems for a one-on-one conference with him. Stanley took my poems, read them, and, taking off his glasses, looked at me and said, "Stop writing about paintings. Write about what's really going on in your life."

It was like having a glass of cold water splashed on my face. It was the truth, but how did he know? I suppose for a writer in his eighties who had been teaching for many years it was obvious. From that conference, and from studying how Stanley Kunitz told the truth in his writing, I learned to write more directly about my life and feelings. Later, I wrote a nonfiction book in an attempt to guide other writers the same way Stanley had guided me. Here is an excerpt from my book *Writing Toward Home: Tales and Lessons to Find Your Way*:

Beginnings

Home is a blueprint of memory. I can draw it for you. Exactly which path went where. Where the creek curved. It's the smell of crayfish and thick mud after a storm. It's jumping on rocks over the creek, sometimes getting my sneakers wet. It's seeking the hiding crayfish.

Something known like breath. Home is what can be recalled without effort—so that sometimes we think, oh, that can't be important. Finding home is crucial to the act of writing. Begin here. With what you know. With the map you've already made in your heart. (1995, 1)

FINDING A HOME IN NONFICTION

Mentor texts help our writers find a home in nonfiction; they also help us find a home teaching it. I've written this book to share the texts, craft tools, and teaching that helped me find a home in nonfiction writing so that you can find one, too. This book is very much a how-to, an action guide to making nonfiction your own. Homes don't merely happen, they result from experiences created when we open ourselves to possibility—when we open our hearts to explore the world around us. So in nonfiction, as in life, home is where our hearts are.

I've designed the parts of *Finding the Heart of Nonfiction* to give you practical guidance first on nonfiction mentor texts themselves, then on integrating them into instruction. Part 1 comprises an introduction to what nonfiction mentor texts are and how to choose them, an overview of ways to use them in the classroom, and tips for how to mine them for nonfiction craft lessons. You'll also find several "Try This" sections, where I suggest some practical tips for how to begin immersing your students in nonfiction mentor texts and creating a nonfiction culture in your classroom.

Part 2 describes seven essential nonfiction craft tools. After a brief introduction to each craft tool, you'll find more Try This sections, which offer practical tips and lessons to help you get your students practicing and deepening their understanding of the craft tools. These sections are often followed by a reproducible collection of relevant excerpts from mentor texts. You can use these reproducibles with your class either as part of the exercises described in the Try This sections or in other ways that make sense to you. You may, of course, decide to create your own collections of mentor texts that are tailored to your students' needs and interests.

Threaded throughout the book, where relevant, you'll find information about ways in which this work helps students meet the Common Core State Standards.

Finally, I've collected some useful tips specific to nonfiction writing in a chapter called "Nuts and Bolts," which addresses not only the variety of nonfiction features your students will encounter as they read nonfiction, and emulate as they write it, but also basics like using quotations and paying attention to passive voice versus active voice.

The craft tools of nonfiction writing allow us to explore our world through writing, engaging not only our minds but our senses and, ultimately, our hearts. I hope that *Finding the Heart of Nonfiction* gives you and your students specific techniques for bringing the same passion and enjoyment to nonfiction that you might experience with fiction or other writing genres.

PART 1

NONFICTION MENTOR TEXTS

Learning to Write from Writers

—⚜—

"Writers learn by emulation."

What Are Mentor Texts?

The word *mentor* comes from the ancient Greek poem *The Odyssey*, by Homer. Mentor was Odysseus' confidante, faithful friend, and reliable steward with whom he entrusted his home and family when he was away on his journeys. And now, of course, the word *mentor* has come to mean someone who imparts wisdom to and shares knowledge with a less experienced colleague.

In a writing community, a mentor text is literature that is used by writers to study craft and genre, and to inspire writing as well as vision. Following are other ways that mentor texts can guide our students' writing.

Mentor Texts

* Mentor texts should be books that students can relate to and can read independently or with some support.

* Mentor texts are to be studied and imitated.

* They serve as exemplars that a writing community can use to study craft, genre, or another aspect of writing.

* They help writers envision the kind of writers they can become.

* They can become coaches and writing partners for writers.

* They serve to show, not just tell, writers how to write well.

Mentor texts are words that writers wish they had written themselves.

Mentor texts are examples of writing that you and your students want to read out loud because you love the way they sound or love the way an author has expressed himself or herself. Mentor texts are words that writers wish they had written themselves.

Collecting a handful of mentor texts, and keeping them as resources for students, is like gathering a multitude of teachers into your classroom.

My Nonfiction Mentor Texts

When I was in school, writing a *nonfiction* report meant copying from an encyclopedia and changing a few words here and there so I didn't get arrested for plagiarism. The writing wasn't mine but instead was a collage of writing from various encyclopedias and books. I didn't know I could write about what I was passionate about and learn to write from studying other writers' words.

Now, my passion for reading nonfiction is deep and ranges from science to autobiography to historical nonfiction.

Three of my favorite nonfiction books of all time are Lewis Thomas' *Late Night Thoughts on Listening to Mahler's Ninth Symphony* (1983); *Bird by Bird: Some Instructions on Writing and Life*, by Anne Lamott (1994); and *John Adams*, by David McCullough (2008). All are written in different subgenres but all are exquisite examples of nonfiction writing. I've learned many lessons about writing from these mentor texts.

Lewis Thomas writes short essays—little vignettes about science topics. I admire how he weaves personal stories with scientific truths and facts. He makes potentially dry subjects fascinating. Lewis Thomas has taught me to write with stories and anecdotes to make writing come alive. He has also taught me to write interesting leads like this one, which begins his chapter about pacemakers, "My Magical Metronome":

> I woke up, late one Friday night, feeling like the Long
> Island Railroad thumping at top speed over a patch of
> bad roadbed. (1983, 45)

Lewis Thomas' essay "Seven Wonders" inspired me to pursue and study the idea of wonder in my son's kindergarten class. This resulted in a book coauthored with my son's former kindergarten teacher, Jen McDonough: *A Place for Wonder: Reading and Writing Nonfiction in the Primary Grades* (2009).

Anne Lamott, on the other hand, is a mentor for totally different reasons. I love her humor, her honesty, and her natural voice. When she writes, it's as if she's speaking directly to me—and I think that every reader feels exactly the same way. *Bird by Bird: Some Instructions on Writing and Life* is one my favorite mentor texts on writing. Here is an excerpt from a chapter on getting started:

> The very first thing I tell my new students on the first day of a workshop is that good writing is about telling the truth. We are a species that needs and wants to understand who we are. Sheep lice do not seem to share this longing, which is one reason they write so very little. But we do. (1994, 3)

Her words make me laugh out loud, but at the same time Anne Lamott imparts essential truths about writing and about life.

And, finally, David McCullough writes passionately about history using imagery, painting distinct and memorable pictures that re-create the historical world he describes. I'm amazed and inspired by his ability to take hundreds of facts and distill them into an engaging narrative. The lead of his biography *John Adams* is one of my favorite beginnings of all time:

> In the cold, nearly colorless light of a New England winter, two men on horseback traveled the coast road below Boston, heading north. A foot or more of snow covered the landscape, the remnants of a Christmas storm that had blanketed Massachusetts from one end of the province to the other. Beneath the snow, after weeks of severe cold, the ground was frozen solid to a depth of two feet. Packed ice in the road, ruts as hard as iron, made the going hazardous, and the riders, mindful of the horses, kept at a walk.
>
> Nothing about the harsh landscape differed from other winters. Nor was there anything to distinguish the two riders, no signs of rank or title, no liveried retinue bringing up the rear. . . .

> He was John Adams of Braintree and he loved to talk.
> He was a known talker. There were some, even among
> his admirers, who wished he talked less. (2008, 17)

I love how he paints the New England winter landscape with words so distinct that I can practically hear the horses' hooves plodding on the packed ice, see the horses' breath billowing in the frigid air, and see the two men riding through the bleak winter landscape. Then, in the third paragraph, McCullough plucks out a singular fact about John Adams and juxtaposes it with the New England landscape: that he loved to talk. The contrast is surprising, and learning this detail about John Adams makes Adams more accessible and human to us.

In addition to these three mentor texts, which I keep on my desk as I write, I have numerous other mentor texts on my bookshelf that I reach for when I need to be inspired.

Types of Nonfiction

In the past, we defined *nonfiction* for our students this way: nonfiction is writing that is true, and fiction is writing that is made up or not true. Over the years, I've come to realize that this definition is way too simplistic and does a disservice to fiction. If you've ever read a novel that brought tears to your eyes, or felt disappointment when you have finished a book because you've longed for more time with the characters, then you know that well-written fiction sometimes feels just as true as nonfiction. We can define fiction as being about imaginary events and people, and nonfiction is writing that deals with facts and gives us information and offers opinions. But both genres need to feel true. Phillip Lopate writes, "When I am writing fiction, I am trying to get at the literary truth; when I am writing nonfiction, I aim for both the literary and literal truth. . . . The materials I am working with in nonfiction are facts and truths" (2013).

The genre of nonfiction is huge and encompasses many subgenres: personal narrative, first-person essay, memoir and autobiography, art review, book review, op-ed, travel writing, and more. In fact, nonfiction is the largest category of any of the writing genres; anything that is not poetry, drama, or fiction is nonfiction. That leaves us with many types of nonfiction. For the sake of simplicity, we can group those types into four main categories, described in more detail in the following sections:

1. Expository, or informative, writing
2. Narrative nonfiction

3. Persuasive, opinion, and argumentative writing

4. Descriptive nonfiction

Expository Writing

Although the purpose of expository writing is to explain, describe, give information, and relay facts to the reader (usually through research), it's rare for such writing not to include nonfiction tools such as narrative and descriptive writing. After all, a list of dates and facts will not engage the reader. A factual report about the first human moon landing might sound like this: "On July 20, 1969, men landed on the moon." But if a writer also includes narrative and descriptive writing, this fact is transformed into writing that comes alive:

> In all directions the land was flat. The horizon was broken only by the rims of distant craters. They could see boulders and ridges. Close at hand, small craters pockmarked the surface; small rocks and pebbles were scattered everywhere.
>
> But Armstrong and Aldrin had to be sure that they had a healthy spacecraft. . . . (Whitehouse 1999)

Narrative nonfiction is a combination of the art of storytelling and journalism.

If students are writing a "research report" or any informative writing, they must figure out how to transfer knowledge so readers can grasp, understand, and even experience the information. In Part 2 in "Turning Facts into Scenes," I discuss specific strategies authors can use to help transfer information so it's dynamic and accessible to readers.

Narrative Nonfiction

What do we mean when we say narrative nonfiction? This genre is the nonfiction category that is closest to fiction—although unlike in fiction, every detail must be factually true. Narrative nonfiction incorporates some of the techniques that a fiction writer might use, such as story or plot, characters, detailed scenes, dialogue, setting, and even sometimes a story arc with a climax and a resolution.

Narrative nonfiction is a combination of the art of storytelling and journalism. Robert Vare writes that narrative nonfiction is an

> attempt to make drama out of the observable world of real people, real places, and real events. It's a sophisticated

form of nonfiction writing, possibly the highest form that harnesses the power of facts to the techniques of fiction constructing a central narrative, setting scenes . . . and, most important, telling the story in a compelling voice that the reader will want to hear. . . . Narrative nonfiction bridges those connections between events that have taken place, and imbues them with meaning and emotion. (2000)

Researchers have found that the human brain has a natural affinity for narrative. We tend to remember facts more accurately if we encounter them in a story rather in a list. Writing narrative, whether it's historical, informational, or journalistic, will help students remember and absorb information and facts.

I've included a list of history and science narrative books in the bibliography (see page 132).

Persuasive, Opinion, and Argumentative Writing

A writer who argues a position or takes a side on an issue is producing persuasive writing to get her point across. Political speeches, op-eds, book reviews, and any article or book that uses facts and opinions to back up a strong point of view is considered persuasive writing, while argumentative writing requires the writer to develop both sides of an issue.

One of my favorite sections of the Sunday newspaper is the op-ed page. I look forward to reading a few favorite guest writers with whom I share the same vision of the world. The heart of persuasive or opinion writing is an idea or an issue that the writer is truly passionate about, and the author must artfully craft the reasons she believes what she believes for the piece to be successful. When we write a persuasive piece, we give an opinion and try to convince the reader to agree. When we write persuasively, here are a few questions we can ask:

* Can the reader tell what I believe?

* What reasons can I give to support my belief or claim?

* Can I make a call to action—is it clear what I want the reader to do?

My eighth-grade son wrote an article for his school newspaper after the presidential election of 2012. Nightly, on the local Florida news station, he would see the lines of people snaking around parking lots and buildings just to be able to cast their votes because Florida legislators cut early voting days, which made the voting sites crowded. When he heard about Desline Victor, the 102-year-old woman who waited in line for three hours to vote, he decided to pick up his pen. This is an excerpt from a longer article that he wrote:

> My opinion about these issues is I think it is unfair that some politicians are doing stuff like this to try and alter whom they want to win the election. I hope that the next election this does not happen, and if it does the Supreme Court should take legal action.

When an eighth-grade boy is compelled to pick up his pen and write about a political injustice, then you know it comes from the heart. In fact, middle school students see injustices all around them every day in school, and persuasive writing is a perfect form for them to express some of their feelings of indignation.

Opinion pieces and persuasive essays must come from the heart; otherwise the writing feels dry and like an assignment.

DESCRIPTIVE NONFICTION

Any nonfiction that uses sensory details, figurative language, and rich detail to portray a scene is using descriptive writing. Travel or nature writing is often in this category because both subgenres depend on description to create a setting and paint a scene.

But any nonfiction should include descriptive writing by using sensory details and figurative language, like this excerpt describing the potentially boring subject of the smallness of a proton, from Bill Bryson's *A Short History of Nearly Everything*:

> Protons are so small that a little dib of ink like the dot on this *i* can hold something in the region of 500,000,000,000 of them. (2004, 9)

The reader can immediately grasp this abstract fact because of the wonderful figurative language Bryson uses.

The term *descriptive writing* is defined as writing that is grounded in observation and experience, which, hopefully, most nonfiction is.

Although it's important to know the four basic nonfiction categories, we should also understand that these categories are not cut-and-dried. If your informative writing

Opinion pieces and persuasive essays must come from the heart; otherwise the writing feels dry and like an assignment.

is just a list of facts, you've lost your reader. Every nonfiction genre should incorporate descriptive writing, and many genres of nonfiction include narrative writing, which helps the reader experience and see the subject of the writing. In Part 2, I identify and describe seven nonfiction craft tools that every nonfiction writer can benefit from, no matter what genre he or she is writing in.

LINKS TO THE COMMON CORE STATE STANDARDS: TYPES OF NONFICTION WRITING

English Language Arts Standards: Writing

The Common Core State Standards emphasize three types of nonfiction writing for students in grades 3–6: opinion, informative/explanatory, and narrative ("real or imagined"). They focus on three types for grades 6–8 as well: argumentative, informative/explanatory, and narrative ("real or imagined").

All emphasis added.

Text Types and Purposes

CCSS.ELA-Literacy.W.3.1: Write **opinion pieces** on topics or texts, supporting a point of view with reasons.

CCSS.ELA-Literacy.W.4.1, 5.1: Write **opinion pieces** on topics or texts, supporting a point of view with reasons and information.

CCSS.ELA-Literacy.W.6.1, 7.1, 8.1: Write **arguments** to support claims with clear reasons and relevant evidence.

CCSS.ELA-Literacy.W.3.2, 4.2, 5.2: Write **informative/explanatory texts** to examine a topic and convey ideas and information clearly.

CCSS.ELA-Literacy.W.6.2, 7.2, 8.2: Write **informative/explanatory texts** to examine a topic and convey ideas, concepts, and information through the selection, organization, and analysis of relevant content.

CCSS.ELA-Literacy.W.3.3, 4.3, 5.3: Write **narratives** to develop real or imagined experiences or events using effective technique, descriptive details, and clear event sequences.

CCSS.ELA-Literacy.W.6.3, 7.3, 8.3: Write **narratives** to develop real or imagined experiences or events using effective technique, relevant descriptive details, and well-structured event sequences.

Literacy in History/Social Studies, Science, and Technical Subjects

CCSS.ELA-Literacy.WHST.6–8.1: Write **arguments** focused on *discipline-specific content.*

CCSS.ELA-Literacy.WHST.6–8.2: Write **informative/explanatory texts**, including the narration of historical events, scientific procedures/experiments, or technical processes.

Choosing Nonfiction Mentor Texts

When I was in school, there were very few nonfiction books written for children. Nonfiction consisted of either textbooks or encyclopedias. Now, when I type "children's nonfiction" into Amazon's search box, approximately 400,000 books come up. Out of the 400,000 children's nonfiction books, I wonder how many of these are well written and possible mentor texts for young writers?

Anthony Fredericks writes, "Not all nonfiction books are satisfactory in terms of information and presentation. They may contain accurate facts, but lack voice and vibrancy. The passions of the writer must come through to support the wonder and awe of the reader" (Fredericks 2003).

One of my favorite books on writing nonfiction is *On Writing Well*, by William Zinsser. I use his description as a guide in choosing mentor texts:

> Ultimately, the product that any writer has to sell is not the subject being written about, but who he or she is. I often find myself reading with interest a topic I never thought would interest me. . . . What holds me is the enthusiasm of the writer for his field.
>
> This is the personal transaction that's at the heart of good nonfiction writing . . . *humanity and warmth*. Good writing has an aliveness that keeps the reader reading

from one paragraph to the next. It's a question of using the English language in a way that will achieve the greatest clarity and strength. (2006, 5; emphasis added)

Those are my favorite criteria for what makes a good a mentor text; humanity and warmth are the essence of good nonfiction. Do the words sound like they were written by an author? Does the text have a voice? Do the words invite the reader in? Do they make the reader feel passionate about or interested in a topic that she didn't care about before?

Think about the nonfiction books in your classroom or school library. How many of them could be mentor texts that fit William Zinsser's description? Some nonfiction books provide good content and may be perfect for research purposes, but as for models for writing that is alive and filled with humanity and warmth, perhaps only 20 percent to 30 percent of your collection meets the criteria.

As your students are browsing through and immersing themselves in nonfiction, ask them to gather books that could be mentor texts and place them in a separate basket or bin in the classroom library. Ask them to think about why a particular nonfiction book should be considered a mentor text. What can this mentor text teach us about writing?

Following are some criteria for choosing mentor texts.

Choosing Mentor Texts

* **Variety of Authors:** Students should be familiar with different authors, from different backgrounds, with different styles.

* **Variety of Language:** Does the writer have a way with words? Do the words create images or bring out the author's voice?

* **Variety of Topics or Ideas:** Is the text about a topic or subject students will connect with, learn from, or find interesting? Does the idea show how writers are inspired by what they see, hear, think, experience, or care about?

* **Variety of Structures and Genres:** Students should be reading in the genre they are writing in. What type of writing is the text? Are features of the genre evident?

* **Books as Models:** Is the text accessible to the students? Will the students be inspired and think, "I can write like that!"?

Try This Modeling with Your Own Mentor Texts

We can share and model the process of finding mentor texts with our students. A mentor text could be a book, poem, essay, article, or any text that has changed our lives, inspired us to become better people, or taught us essential craft writing lessons.

After sharing your own mentor text, ask students to each select a text that has inspired them personally or taught them something about writing. It could be a nonfiction mentor text if students have been immersed in nonfiction, or it could be a text in any genre. Here are some criteria they could be thinking about as they select their mentor texts:

- ✦ A mentor text could be by an author with whom students share the same vision of the world.
- ✦ A mentor text could have writing that they think is beautiful and that they admire, and that they perhaps would like to imitate.
- ✦ A mentor text could have writing that they think is unique—an example of craft that they find surprising or interesting.

Reading with a vision of learning how to write from other writers requires students to shift from how they might usually read. When we read fiction, we usually read for story and character; when we read nonfiction, we tend to read for information or admire the striking graphics or colorful photos. Putting on the lens of a writer reading for inspiring writing that will teach him to do *his* best writing will be a new way of reading for many students.

A minilesson to introduce students to the idea of mentor texts might go like this:

> *I brought one of my favorite books with me today. This book is what I call a* mentor text. *Does anyone know what a mentor text is?*

Don't be surprised if your students don't know what a mentor text is even though you might have discussed it with them previously. In one class, a boy raised his hand and said that he thought a mentor text was a book with different kinds of fonts. A girl in the same class said, "Oh, I thought it was a kind of fish." This was despite the fact that there were bins labeled "Mentor Texts" containing magnificent books in the classroom library, and the wonderful teacher had discussed what a mentor text was during writing minilessons.

> *A mentor text is a book that teaches me something about writing, or inspires me to write, or sometimes even teaches me an interesting way to look at the world.*

The word mentor comes from one of the longest poems ever writ-
ten, called The Odyssey. Odysseus, the main character of the poem,
leaves home to go on a long journey. He leaves his house and family
in the care of his friend and teacher, a guy named Mentor. Mentor is
a very wise man and has taught Odysseus a lot of wise things. So, the
word mentor means a kind of teacher. And a mentor text is a book, or
any piece, that teaches us something about writing.

Share your own mentor text and be specific about what the book has taught you about writing.

My mentor text is a biography of President John Adams by David
McCullough. He is a history writer and one of the things I've learned
from him is to paint pictures with words. Listen to how he paints
pictures with words in the first sentence of his lead. You might want
to close your eyes as I read to see if you can picture it:

> In the cold, nearly colorless light of a New England winter, two men
> on horseback traveled the coast road below Boston, heading north.
> (2008, 17)

I have a lot of books that are mentor texts. A mentor text is
different from a book that just has a good story or pictures. It's a
book or poem or any piece of writing that teaches you something
about writing.

I'd like you to think right now about a book that you may have
read or heard your teacher read that is a mentor text—a book that
has taught you something about writing.

You might have to model what a mentor text is several times. Students initially think that because they like a story or photos in a nonfiction book, it's a mentor text. Often, when students share mentor texts, they begin recalling the plot or share an amazing photo of, for example, a snake. You can turn that sharing around by saying, "If you were writing your own nonfiction book, what could this book teach you that you could use as a writer?"

Student Examples

In the following examples, third-grade students hadn't started their immersion in nonfiction so most of the students chose fiction mentor texts. See page 19 for a reproducible copy of the note-taking sheet students used.

I love how this third grader, Carson, writes about the ending in *Diary of a Wimpy Kid* (Kinney 2007): "and around the end there's a smack boom in your face ending 1,000 times different from the beginning."

He wrote that he learned about *voice content* as a writing craft tool, and when I asked him what voice content was, he explained it this way: "It's when the writer talks with voice that sounds like somebody is really talking." Notice the excellent example from *Diary of a Wimpy Kid* that he gives.

You can tell by Nicole's example (next page) that Kristin Ackerman, their wonderful third-grade teacher, had taught a craft lesson on internal thought, and that Nicole was able to identify internal thought in her mentor text *The Baby-Sitters Club: The Truth About Stacey* (Telgemeier and Martin 2006).

When I talked to Logan about why he chose *Nurse, Soldier, Spy: The Story of Sarah Edwards, a Civil War Hero* (Moss 2011) as his mentor text, he began to tell me the plot of the book, which is very typical for most readers and writers. Again, because his teacher, Kristin Ackerman, had done an outstanding job teaching her students writing craft tools, Logan was able to name several craft tools: "I learned multiple fonts, one thing, leads, stretching the truth, and a sign instead of pictures."

My Mentor Text

Title: *Diary of a wimpy kid*

Author: *Jeff Kenny*

Why did you choose this book as a mentor text?:

Because the book uses lots of voice and around the end theres a smack boom in your face ending 1,000 times different from the begining also the book continues the story in pictures sometimes,

What writing craft tools has this mentor text taught you?

Comical writing and through out the entire book voice content.

Please write down one example of incredible writing.

Ok so maybe I was exagerating on the dad not being mad thing because when I got home—

My Mentor Text

Title: The baby sitters club

Author: Raina

1. Why did you choose this book as a mentor text?:
I choosed it because it has a lot of internal thought

2. What writing craft tools has this mentor text taught you?
It taught me that we can always put internal thought in your writing piece.

3. Please write down one example of incredible writing.
Like their was once when MaryAnne was in her room studying she couldn't stop thinking about her fight that she got in with her friends. Here are a few things she said: "I couldn't concentrate on my homework, I wish I hadn't said all those things to my friends. But they said mean things about ME, too.

When I questioned Logan about what "one thing" meant, he showed me how on each page the author focused on one moment rather than a bunch of different topics. He then showed me what he meant when he said "a sign instead of pictures" and how the illustrator used signs as clues instead of pictures.

Begin your discussion of mentor texts early on in the school year—perhaps on nonfiction Monday (see page 30). Each time you give a writing minilesson, and use a text as an example, refer to the text as a *mentor text*. Keep a basket or bin of special books that become class mentor texts.

Studying the writing of a favorite nonfiction author as part of a genre study is another way to introduce the idea of reading like a writer.

My Mentor Text

Title: NURSE SOLDIER SPY

Author:

Why did you choose this book as a mentor text?:
it teeches you the History I like it because it is a girl and she went in the aremy.

What writing craft tools has this mentor text taught you?
I learnd multiple fonts, one thing leads and strechting the truth a sine insted of a paragraf

My Mentor Text Note-Taking Sheet

Name: _____

Title: _____

Author: _____

Why is this book a mentor text?

_____

_____

_____

_____

_____

_____

What writing craft tools has this mentor text taught you?

_____

_____

_____

_____

_____

_____

Please write down one example of incredible writing.

_____

_____

_____

_____

_____

_____

Reading Nonfiction
with Different Lenses

In *The Reader, the Text, the Poem: The Transactional Theory of the Literary Work,* Louise M. Rosenblatt (1985) proposes that there are two kinds of reader-and-text transactions: efferent and aesthetic. An efferent reading stance asks students to read for information and to analyze and synthesize that information. An aesthetic stance involves reading with a focus on feelings, thoughts, and images; the reader shapes meaning from the text through personal experiences and emotions as well as from noticing the aesthetic or artistic quality of a text. Of course, when we read nonfiction we read with a blend of the two stances: we can learn information from reading nonfiction but we can also pay attention to our personal response as well as our aesthetic experience. Our goal is for students to read nonfiction with both an efferent and an aesthetic stance.

I'm reminded of a boy who entered a first-grade classroom breathless one morning because he needed to find out exactly what food to feed his new pet snail that he found on the sidewalk outside of his house. When the teacher gave him a book that would help him, it wasn't literary nonfiction; it was a how-to-take-care-of-your-pet-snail kind of book that could answer his question, What do snails eat? He didn't linger over the beautiful language or the imagery, he didn't savor the words the author used to describe the snail, nor did he think to himself, "That's an amazing lead." He skimmed the book for the information he needed to keep his snail alive, and once he found it, he put the book down—his reading was finished. This book would probably not be considered a mentor text. This young boy was reading with an efferent stance: he was reading for information. The world of nonfiction is vast, and there are many times when reading nonfiction demands reading with an efferent stance.

In contrast, the responses by third graders on the mentor text note-taking sheets in the previous Try This section are all examples of reading with an aesthetic stance—relishing the craft tools that the authors used to help make writing come alive.

Nonfiction is vast, and there are many times when reading nonfiction demands reading with an efferent stance.

Try This Using Different Lenses to Read

Following is an excerpt describing how sea horses eat. After you have explained to students the two types of reading stances, ask them to try reading the passage with an efferent stance first (i.e., for information). See what information they can glean from this passage:

> Sea horses eat by suction feeding. A complex network of interconnected bones pulled by several muscles creates suction force directed at prey and the surrounding water. They draw water containing their prey into their mouths, from where it is diverted into the esophagus for digestion. (wiki.answers.com)

As you read the text aloud, ask students to pay attention first to what information they find in this passage. They may notice the following facts:

- ✦ Sea horses eat by suction feeding.
- ✦ Bones and muscles give sea horses suction.
- ✦ Sea horses suck the water containing their prey into their mouths.
- ✦ Water goes from the mouth to the esophagus for digestion.

Then ask your students to try reading the same passage with an aesthetic stance. Ask them to focus on the images; any interesting words the author used; examples of figurative language; and anything else they notice about the way the text is crafted.

> Sea horses eat by suction feeding. A complex network of interconnected bones pulled by several muscles creates suction force directed at prey and the surrounding water. They draw water containing their prey into their mouths, from where it is diverted into the esophagus for digestion.

It's difficult for me to do an aesthetic reading of this text (and it will be difficult for students as well). Sure, some of the words are specific (*draw water, diverted*) but for the most part, the language in this text is abstract, and the author's voice is flat. This passage is missing Zinsser's criteria for excellent nonfiction writing: aliveness, warmth, and humanity.

In contrast, below is another passage taken from a nonfiction picture book on sea horses called *Sea Horse: The Shyest Fish in the Sea*, by Chris Butterworth (2006). Ask your students to try reading the passage first with an efferent stance, looking for information. (I've kept the original picture book word spacing.)

> This new sea horse
> is only as long
> as your eyelash,
> but she can find her
> own food right away.
> Her eyes move separately
> from each other
> (one can peer up while
> the other looks down),
> so she can spot
> food coming from
> any direction.
>
> With one quick slurp,
> she sucks her catch
> into the end
> of her snout and
> swallows it whole—
> sea horses don't have teeth.

I can identify several pieces of information from this passage:

+ Baby sea horses can find their own food right away.
+ Sea horses' eyes move up and down separately so they can spot food from any direction.
+ Sea horses suck their prey whole into their snouts.
+ Sea horses don't have teeth.

Now, ask your students to try reading this same passage with an aesthetic stance, paying attention to the imagery, word choice, figurative language, and so on.

> This new sea horse
> is only as long
> as your eyelash,
> but she can find her
> own food right away.
> Her eyes move separately

from each other
(one can peer up while
the other looks down),
so she can spot
food coming from
any direction.

With one quick slurp,
she sucks her catch
into the end
of her snout and
swallows it whole—
sea horses don't have teeth.

I can get my students started by modeling what I notice when reading the passage with an aesthetic stance and then asking them to take over:

> I notice the beautiful and precise simile that Chris Butterworth uses to describe the size of a baby sea horse: "This new sea horse is only as long as your eyelash."
>
> By using a simile of an eyelash instead of just saying, "Baby sea horses are really small," she shows me exactly how small a baby sea horse is.
>
> I also notice the active and vivid verbs that this author uses:
>
> - one can **peer** up
> - she can **spot**
> - she **sucks** her catch
>
> Peer, spot, sucks—these are such precise verbs that show us exactly how sea horses eat. She didn't just say, "Sea horses eat their catch." I can picture a sea horse moving its eyes up and down and slurping its prey into its snout.

If I were using *Sea Horse: The Shyest Fish in the Sea* as a mentor text, these are three possible minilessons I would give my students on nonfiction writing:

- ✦ using figurative language (simile) in nonfiction
- ✦ using precise, vivid, active verbs
- ✦ using imagery

Ways to Include Nonfiction
Mentor Texts in the Classroom

There are three primary ways to include mentor texts in the classroom:

1. Read-aloud and immersion
2. Student nonfiction mentor text anthologies
3. Minilessons on specific craft tools (see Part 2)

READ-ALOUD AND IMMERSION

If we want our students to write high-quality nonfiction we must read aloud—and provide time for browsing and sharing well-written nonfiction books.

We can select a few superb examples of nonfiction writing and read aloud excerpts, choosing our favorite parts—a lead, a beautiful sentence, an interesting way the author expressed something. Or we can read aloud an entire nonfiction book, particularly if it's a narrative or filled with descriptive writing. Listening to nonfiction tunes students' ears to the music and voice of excellent nonfiction. William Zinsser writes, "Find the best writers in the fields that interest you and read their work aloud. Get their voice and their taste into your ear—their attitude toward language" (2006, 236).

We also need to get well-written nonfiction texts in students' hands and let them browse, savor, and become familiar with them. We have to remember that vibrant pictures and graphics don't necessarily make for a well-written mentor text. During this time students are reading like writers, with an aesthetic stance, and not engaging in research yet. The distinction is subtle but important.

As you read nonfiction aloud or as students browse nonfiction, ask them to jot down one or two things they notice about the writing.

* What interesting language or word choice does the author use? (sensory details; precise, specific vocabulary; vivid or striking words; figurative language; etc.)

* What do you notice about the way the sentences are structured? (paragraphs; short versus long; etc.)

* How is the writing organized? (chapters; chronological order; question and answer; circular; compare and contrast; etc.)

* What are your favorite parts of the mentor text? Why?

We have to remember that vibrant pictures and graphics don't necessarily make for a well-written mentor text.

When choosing mentor texts for read-alouds and for immersion, try to choose trade books written by "real" authors rather than books written and produced for publishing companies' reading series, which often lack voice and Zinsser's "aliveness."

Why Use Books Written by Real Authors?

* **Author's Voice:** We want our students to read nonfiction that has been written and crafted by a nonfiction author with a unique voice that we can recognize over subsequent readings of his or her books.

* **Author's Point of View:** We want our students to read nonfiction that has been written and crafted by a nonfiction author with a distinct point of view.

* **Author's Craft:** We want our students to be able to study and learn from an author's craft.

* **Author's Life and Process:** Students can learn from studying a nonfiction author's life: how he or she became a nonfiction author; how he or she goes about researching and writing books; what his or her process of writing is. We want to build a culture of nonfiction readers and writers in the classroom and to understand an author's process and vision because it personalizes nonfiction for students.

When we choose real books written by real authors, our students develop a sense of nonfiction mentor texts as having been crafted by living, breathing people. As students interact with mentor texts in your classroom, you may want to have them consider these questions about the authors:

* Why did the author become a nonfiction writer?

* What's the author's process of researching and writing?

* Does the author have a unique style of writing? Or perhaps a unique point of view?

When we choose real books written by real authors, our students develop a sense of nonfiction mentor texts as having been crafted by living, breathing people.

STUDENT NONFICTION ANTHOLOGIES

As we make our thinking about mentor texts public and give students ample opportunities to hear nonfiction read aloud and read independently, we can begin to ask students to create their own mentor text anthologies. This gradual release of responsibility will support their efforts to learn about writing from other writers.

Try This Creating Nonfiction Mentor Text Anthologies

Jen McDonough and Kristin Ackerman, two incredible teachers of first and third graders, invite students to create their own mentor text anthologies. For example, when Jen or Kristin gives a minilesson on a particular craft such as leads, students will then search for leads they admire and copy these examples into their anthologies, along with samples from their own writing. In Kristin's class, students become experts at a particular craft tool. Here are a few suggestions for creating mentor text anthologies:

+ Mentor text anthologies can be composition notebooks, spiral notebooks, or handmade notebooks tied together with string (see page 29).

+ Mentor text anthologies can contain multiple genres or focus on a particular genre such as nonfiction.

+ Students can hand copy or machine copy excerpts from books. Be sure to ask them to write the title and author of the book from which each excerpt came.

+ Students can also include samples from their own writing.

Student Examples

In the examples on the following pages, the third graders searched and found mentor texts on a variety of different craft tools, including transition words.

This third grader, Spencer, searched and found a "setting" lead from *Fireflies!* by Julie Brinckloe (1986), and then he wrote his own (see "Leads: The Doorway into Writing" on page 60).

Another student author, Spencer, used Julie Brinckloe's *Fireflies!* (1986) as a mentor text and copied the last line as an example of "endings with feeling" (see "Endings: Letting Words Linger" on page 103).

Even transition words such as *in addition, not only, another thing, also* and *well* are craft tools that students can learn in a minilesson and then find examples of in mentor texts such as Jacob did in his mentor text anthology. (See "Links to the Common Core State Standards: Transition Words and Phrases" on page 118.)

Strong Leads

Setting

On a summer evening
I looked up from dinner,
through the open window

My mom is asleep and
my Dad is working in a
room somewhere in a secret
room. I'm alone. shadows
are creeping along the
wall. And It's raining and
the clouds are on the ground.
And It's damp outside. It's
creepy . . . "BOY, this is

Endings

①Endings with feeling
The moonlight and the
fire flies swam in my
tears,
but I could feel myself
smiling

Transitions

In addition,
Not only,
onuther thing,

Also, pigs *absolutely refuse* to wear majorette uniforms.

Well, forget it. Pigs don't care about floats.

Try This Fitting It All in with Nonfiction Mondays

How do you fit all of this nonfiction work in? Here's one idea. Across the United States teachers are devoting one day a week to nonfiction. Teachers' blogs in the KidLitosphere (www.kidlitosphere.org/) devote Mondays (though it could be any day that works for you) to the study and celebration of nonfiction, complete with reviews of new nonfiction books, teaching ideas, and interviews with nonfiction authors. Instead of scheduling a monthlong nonfiction unit of study, you might try introducing nonfiction once a week throughout the year, taking advantage of having consistent weekly opportunities to immerse kids in the genre of nonfiction.

One of my favorite children's literature blogs is Franki Sibberson and Mary Lee Hahn's blog *A Year of Reading*. Here is an excerpt of an entry about getting nonfiction books in the hands of Franki's students:

Nonfiction: An Update

I posted in early December about my plans to make December a month of nonfiction reading. I had big goals for my students and met many of them. The process took a little longer than I planned and much of the month was spent finding great books, building stamina for nonfiction, etc. I was getting a bit discouraged but then I started noticing things. I noticed a child hand off a nonfiction book to another child as they were lining up for lunch. I noticed a few books begin to circulate and become popular in the classroom. I noticed some readers stick with a topic. I noticed kids finding series or authors that they wanted to read more of. . . .

I have a group of kids reading lots about baseball history. These books seem to be circulating between 5–6 kids in the classroom. The books they are currently reading include:

We Are the Ship: The Story of Negro League Baseball by Kadir Nelson

Home Run: The Story of Babe Ruth by Robert Burleigh

Henry Aaron's Dream by Matt Tavares

Heroes of Baseball: The Men Who Made It America's Favorite Game by Robert Lipsyte

(http://readingyear.blogspot.com/2013/01/nonfiction-update.html)

Try setting aside at least thirty minutes every Monday for nonfiction. During this time you can do the following:

+ read aloud

+ have students browse nonfiction books

+ have students browse bookmarked websites of nonfiction authors

For example, on his website, author Nic Bishop discusses three ways he gathers information for his beautifully written and self-photographed nonfiction books:

> **How I Research My Books**
>
> The first [source] is information that I learnt during the years that I studied biology. . . .
>
> My second source of information is perhaps the most interesting—first hand observation. Because I take photographs, I become more involved in my books than if I were just to write them. . . . But as a photographer, I have to spend five or six months in close contact with my animal subjects. . . . And during these months of photography, I learn so many things about my subjects by first hand observation, which in turn inform my text. . . .
>
> Of course, I also do my fair share of book research in order to gather information. (www.nicbishop.com/nic_bishop_029.htm)

Knowing that Nic Bishop's firsthand close observation of his subjects plays an important role in his writing can inspire students to also use firsthand observation as one way to research their nonfiction topics.

As you're in the immersion phase of exploring nonfiction, keep a chart titled "What We Notice About Nonfiction." Make a two-column chart with a list of text features on one side and a list of craft features on the other side:

WHAT WE NOTICE ABOUT NONFICTION

Craft Features	**Text Features**
Uses concrete nouns	Photographs/illustrations and captions
Uses active verbs	Index
Groups related information together	Charts and graphs

Favorite Nonfiction Authors for Children

There are scores of wonderful authors writing nonfiction for children. Here is a list of some of my favorite science authors:

- Laurence Pringle
- Diane Swanson
- Nic Bishop
- Gail Gibbons
- Seymour Simon
- Franklyn Branley
- Patricia Lauber
- Aliki
- Linda Glaser
- Melissa Stewart
- Sy Montgomery
- Dianna Hutts Aston
- Joanne Ryder
- Nicola Davies
- Chris Butterworth
- Peter Lourie

These are some of my favorite history and social studies authors:

- Patricia Polacco
- Candace Fleming
- Marc Aronson
- Kathryn Lasky
- Kadir Nelson
- Russell Freedman
- Jan Greenberg

Mining Mentor Texts for Craft
Teaching Possibilities

As students begin their study of nonfiction, ask yourself, "What do my students need in terms of writing craft lessons? Which mentor texts would be good examples of nonfiction craft that I could share during my minilessons and conferences?" Once you've identified several mentor texts, you can ask of each one, "What teaching possibilities does this mentor text hold? Can I teach several minilessons from this one text?"

For example, let's look at the opening of a picture book biography called *Henry Aaron's Dream*, by Matt Tavares (2012), and think about what teaching possibilities the text holds. As you read the excerpt, ask yourself, "What writing minilessons could I teach from this text?"

> **Henry Aaron had a dream.**
> He wanted to be a big-league baseball player.
>
> He didn't have a bat,
> so he'd swing a broom handle
> or a stick
> or whatever he could find.
>
> Henry didn't have a baseball, either,
> so he'd hit bottle caps

> or tie a few old rags together
> or crumple up a tin can.
>
> Henry liked to play in his yard
> and imagine himself in the big leagues.
>
> But his father knew he shouldn't get his hopes up.
> "Ain't no colored ballplayers," he told Henry.
>
> Still, Henry held onto his dream.

Tavares uses *dialogue* to show Henry Aaron's father's character and give us a historical context:

> "Ain't no colored ballplayers," he told Henry.

The *specific and concrete nouns* let the reader picture the objects that Henry Aaron used instead of a ball:

> so he'd hit bottle caps
> or tie a few old rags together
> or crumple up a tin can.

By *repeating* the line "Henry Aaron had a dream" at the beginning and end of the first page ("Still, Henry held onto his dream."), Tavares shows us how Henry Aaron held onto his dream no matter what obstacles were in his way and adds a musical and pattern element to the text.

When you read students' writing and when you confer with them, ask yourself these questions:

* What specific craft lesson can I teach this student that will help her writing?

* What mentor text would be an excellent example of that specific craft tool that I can show to my student?

* What teaching possibilities does this text hold that will help my students as writers?

* What craft features can I identify, name, and chart from the mentor texts? How can I use these anchor charts throughout the nonfiction genre study?

* After I read aloud a mentor text and give a minilesson on a specific craft element, can I make similar mentor texts available for students to read?

* Can I compare mentor texts and authors within the same genre?

In Part 2, I examine seven important craft tools and show ways to use nonfiction mentor texts to teach our students how to incorporate those craft tools into their own nonfiction writing.

PART 2

TEACHING 7 NONFICTION CRAFT TOOLS WITH MENTOR TEXTS

*"Good writing is good writing
no matter what genre you're writing in."*

Keep It Simple

I'm fond of the expression *You can't see the forest for the trees*. The older I get, the more complicated life seems—especially with the onslaught of email, texting, Facebook, and so on. I am a believer in simplicity, or at least simplicity as a goal. I believe simplicity can be a goal for teaching writing as well. There are so many hundreds of books, blogs, websites, and articles about how to teach writing that it's easy to get overwhelmed and lose sight of the big picture: good writing is good writing no matter what genre you're writing in, and I believe that there are only a handful of fundamental craft tools that apply to any genre.

After working with students on nonfiction writing, and thinking about what's essential as I write my own nonfiction, I've come to believe that there are seven craft lessons that are essential tools for writing nonfiction:

1. Focus: the hearth of nonfiction writing
2. Turning facts into scenes: writing with imagery
3. Leads: the doorway into writing
4. Point of view and voice: who are we when we write?
5. Precise language: details, details, and more details
6. Text structures: writing bird by bird
7. Endings: letting words linger

Of course there's more to writing nonfiction than knowing craft tools. Depending on the genre of nonfiction, it can require researching, analyzing, and pulling from many different sources. It requires gathering facts—dates, minute details, and bits of information. It requires an understanding of theories that build a nonfiction text up brick by brick and make it verifiable. It also requires the ability to stand back and reflect on what the big picture or idea is. Writers of nonfiction need time to dig deep, time to write and rewrite, and time to study other writers to see how they did it.

Learning from the NCTE Orbis Pictus Award for Outstanding Nonfiction for Children

The criteria for the NCTE Orbis Pictus Award for Outstanding Nonfiction for Children (www.ncte.org/awards/orbispictus) can serve as a guide for teaching and assessing students' nonfiction writing. Some of the writing criteria for the Orbis Pictus Award are as follows:

Accuracy

- facts current and complete
- balance of fact and theory
- stereotypes avoided
- authenticity of detail

Organization

- logical development
- clear sequence
- patterns provided (general-to-specific, simple-to-complex, etc.)

Style

- writing is . . . stimulating
- reveals author's enthusiasm for subject
- curiosity and wonder encouraged
- appropriate terminology
- rich language
- model exemplary expository writing

I. Focus

The Hearth of Nonfiction Writing

Good writing comes down to one word: *focus*. It's interesting that the word *focus* didn't originally relate to a camera but instead was the Latin word for *hearth*, a place in the home where family and friends come together to warm and comfort themselves. If we think of focus in writing in the same way—the hearth of a piece of writing around which all the details and words gather—it's a helpful metaphor. But finding the focus in any genre, nonfiction included, is one of the biggest challenges writers face.

One of the keys to writing quality nonfiction is being able to distill a lot of information and details into a focused text. William Zinsser reminds us to think small. He writes, "Decide what corner of your subject you're going to bite off, and be content to cover it well and stop" (2006, 52). Don't try to write the entire city block, or even half a city block, but just a piece of it—a corner.

One of the most difficult things about focusing nonfiction, particularly after researching and gathering numerous facts about a topic, is distilling a wealth of information down to what's essential. One of the biggest challenges for nonfiction writers is trying to explain complex issues in two- to three-page essays, or feature articles, or even thirty-two-page nonfiction picture books.

Roy Peter Clark (2013b), the founder of the Poynter Institute, refers to CBS radio correspondent Peter King, who had to take long reports from NASA and distill them into 30-second on-air reports. One strategy Clark suggests is to think of non-fiction writing as a picture postcard. "Look how little space you have to convey a message to a friend from a distant location, maybe the Leaning Tower of Pisa. There's an image on the front that gives you a sense of place, but the writing has to be highly selective, to make the best possible point in the least amount of space."

He gives us other strategies to think of when we're trying to distill a lot of information, such as "Ask yourself, 'What information can I afford to leave out?' Focus—that is, zero in." Clark goes on to say that many of his journalism students would tell him lots of interesting facts and details but, he said, "It was like a bunch of pearls without the string to turn them into a necklace."

William Zinsser writes:

> By far the biggest problem was compression: how to dis-till a coherent narrative from a huge and tangled mass of experiences and feelings and memories. "I want to write an article about the disappearance of small towns in Iowa," one woman told us, describing how the fabric of life in the Midwest had frayed since she was a girl on her grandparent's farm. . . . But nobody can write a decent article about the disappearance of small towns in Iowa; it would be all generalization and no humanity. The writer would have to write about one small town in Iowa and thereby tell her larger story, and even within that one town she would have to reduce her story still further: to one store, or one family, or one farmer. (2006, 256)

In the early stages of research or writing, students should be thinking about their focus so that their research and writing will support it.

In the early stages of research or writing, students should be thinking about their focus so that their research and writing will support it. Students should ask themselves questions like "What do I want readers to remember the most about my piece? What point do I really want to make?"

Here are seven strategies that help nonfiction writers focus their topics:

1. Ask questions
2. Focus on your interests and passions
3. Find your purpose and audience
4. Study mentor texts
5. Distill information into six-word memoirs
6. Study nonfiction titles
7. Write a poem

ASK QUESTIONS

Asking questions can help us focus a big topic. We can ask ourselves: "What do I really want to say? What do I think or believe about my topic? What am I curious about? What do I wonder?"

If my topic is, for example, the ocean, one question I have is How and why do ocean waves continually roll into shore without ever stopping? I know a little bit about waves from taking Oceanography 101 in college—that their motion has to do with gravity and Earth's rotation—but there is a lot more I'd like to know. Asking that one question about the waves has helped focus my topic, make it more concise.

I also warn students not to choose questions that lead to a slight and insignificant focus. For example, I might ask a question like How many waves break on shore every day? But for one thing, I'm not sure if that is an answerable question, and for another, if answerable, the question would lead to a small, finite answer rather than a focused yet rich topic. Encourage your students to try to reach a happy medium.

FOCUS ON YOUR INTERESTS AND PASSION

Paying attention to what element of a larger topic we're really interested in and passionate about can also help us find focus. We can ask: "What really interests me about this topic? What do I feel passionate about? What do I really think about this subject?"

Nonfiction writer Melissa Stewart calls this focus driven by a writer's passion the "creative core" while Candace Fleming (2011), another excellent nonfiction writer, identifies it as the "vital idea." Stewart writes, "It's the heart of a great nonfiction manuscript. It's what a specific author brings to a topic . . . that no one else can. It's why a topic chooses an author, not the other way around" (2012).

Another potential focus for my ocean example, driven by my passionate curiosity about this subject, might be deep-sea creatures—the ones with no eyes that live in perpetual darkness. Someone else might be interested in a completely different ocean-related topic like sharks or jellyfish. Our interests can guide our focus and lead the exploration of our topic.

Our interests can guide our focus and lead the exploration of our topic.

FIND YOUR PURPOSE AND AUDIENCE

Understanding the purpose and the audience of our writing can also help us focus. If, for example, I want to write a newspaper article to persuade people to pressure BP to set more stringent drilling regulations so as to avoid another oil spill in the Gulf of Mexico, my focus will be very different than if I am writing a nonfiction piece that explores how ocean waves work, or an informational text about deep-sea creatures.

STUDY MENTOR TEXTS

Studying the ways that other authors focus their topics can help us get ideas for focusing our own pieces.

In the picture book biography *The Watcher: Jane Goodall's Life with the Chimps*, Jeanette Winter writes the following in the end section called "A Note About This Story":

> To simplify the story, I focused solely on Jane's own ac-
> complishments. I omitted mention of her married life,
> her son, and her mother's unwavering support.
>
> I wish when I was a little girl, I could have read about
> someone like Jane Goodall—a brave woman who wasn't
> afraid to do something that had never been done before.
> So now I've made this book for that little girl, who still
> speaks to me. (2011)

Jeanette Winter eliminated many details from Goodall's life because they didn't support the focus of her story. Winter's wish to have been inspired by someone like Jane Goodall when she was a girl is her "creative core," as Melissa Stewart calls it, or her "vital idea," as Candace Fleming writes—and the heart of her biography.

DISTILL INFORMATION

When I think about nonfiction writing, I think about gold miners—just think how much sand a gold miner had to sift through, for days and days, to find even one gold nugget. Just like gold miners, nonfiction writers need to sift through an abundance of information, research, knowledge, and expertise about our topics: How do we know which pieces are important enough to keep? Which pieces are gold nuggets and which are sand?

Once we identify a focus, then we can hold on to all of the supporting facts— the gold nuggets—and let the rest go. If we don't distill information, we give every fact and detail the same importance, leading to a piece that feels diffuse and unfocused.

Try This Distilling Information into a Six-Word Memoir

One exercise that helps students learn the process of synthesizing copious amounts of information is writing a six-word memoir, or biography—similar to Roy Peter Clark's strategy of thinking about what few things you should write to a friend on a picture postcard.

Synthesizing a lot of information is especially difficult when writing biography and autobiography because it means extracting what's essential about someone's whole life—or even more difficult, one's own life. That's why so many students begin autobiographies with the date and place where they were born: "On January 27, 1999, I was born in New York Hospital," and so on. It's a simple, known fact and easily accessible.

In this exercise, first ask students to brainstorm a few essential truths about themselves and their lives. Then ask them to reflect on these essential truths and condense one or more of them into a six-word memoir. The six words shouldn't be a known fact like "I was born in New York," but instead something deeper, emotional or self-revealing.

Following are a few criteria for writing a six-word memoir, or a six-word biography:

+ Your memoir or biography must capture an essential essence, or an important detail about you, or your subject—not just a known fact.

+ Ask yourself, "What do I really want to say about my life (or the life of my biographical subject)?"

+ Write about a hidden part of yourself, or your subject—something that no one else knows.

+ Write about a feeling you have about yourself, or your subject.

If a student is writing a six-word biography about John Adams, for example, he shouldn't just write a well-known fact, like "The second president of America." Instead, he should write a character trait like David McCullough did in *John Adams*: "John Quincy Adams loved to talk" (2008, 17).

Here are a few examples of six-word memoirs written by fifth-grade students from The Bronx Charter School for Better Learning under the guidance of their wonderful teacher, Bruce Ballard:

Sick of being a middle child.—Kevin

Life is boring without a dad.—Keshawn

Earthquake shook Haiti. Earthquake shook me.—Kimberly

You're young, then old, really old.—Maya

I believe that one of the reasons these students were so successful in writing their six-word memoirs was because they had been reading and writing poetry, which by its very nature makes a big emotional impact using the least amount of words.

Each one of these six-word memoirs, or six-word biographies, can be turned into chapters in longer, more substantial memoirs, autobiographies, or biographies.

Try This Studying Titles to Learn About Focus

Oftentimes you can tell the focus of a topic by reading a text's title. All the examples here are about the ocean, but you can try this minilesson with any topic that the class is studying in science or social studies or any topic that the class is interested in. Select texts that show multiple ways authors have focused on one topic. Remember that the texts you choose don't have to be books; they can also be magazine articles or even poems.

Let's look at the titles in the following list to study how several authors focused their nonfiction texts about the ocean. When you do this work with students, encourage them to try to identify the focus of each text just by reading the title:

> *Sounds of the Wild: Ocean*, by Maurice Pledger
>
> *Oceans: Dolphins, Sharks, Penguins, and More!* by Johnna Rizzo
>
> *Hello Ocean*, by Pam Muñoz Ryan

Your students may notice that we can surmise, just by looking at the title, what the focus of *Sounds of the Wild: Ocean* is. The book will take us beneath the water's surface to listen to ocean creatures' sounds.

Johnna Rizzo introduces us to the ocean through a few of its most popular creatures in *Oceans: Dolphins, Sharks, Penguins, and More!*

Pam Muñoz Ryan's title *Hello Ocean* doesn't clearly describe the book's focus; its title is more representative of its poetic form, which shows us the beauty of the ocean through our five senses.

You can guide your students to notice how each one of these authors had to make a decision about what small corner of his or her big topic, the ocean, the author wanted to explore. For more practice with this, you might ask students to read the titles of the following texts. None of the texts is an all-about book; each has a specific focus that is evident by reading its title. Ask the kids, "Can you identify what the focus of each text is by reading its title?"

> *The Watcher: Jane Goodall's Life with the Chimps*, by Jeanette Winter
>
> *The Man Who Made Time Travel*, by Kathryn Lasky

Winter's Tail: How One Little Dolphin Learned to Swim Again, by Juliana Hatkoff, Isabella Hatkoff, and Craig Hatkoff

The Case of the Vanishing Golden Frogs: A Scientific Mystery, by Sandra Markle

As your students are researching and preparing to write their own nonfiction pieces, you might encourage them to brainstorm specific titles for their pieces first. If a student can't think of an accurate title, sometimes it's because she hasn't found her focus yet.

WRITING TIP

Narrowing in on a Focused Title

When a student knows what her topic is, she should try writing a list of three possible titles, starting with a general title and then focusing more and more specifically.

For example, this book had a progression of titles from general to more focused:

1. *Nonfiction Writing*
2. *Nonfiction Craft Tools and Mentor Texts*
3. *Finding the Heart of Nonfiction: Teaching 7 Essential Craft Tools with Mentor Texts*

Try This Writing a Poem to Help Focus a Topic

Poetry is by its nature distilled and focused. Ironically, the more general and universal a poem is, the less successful it is. Writing a poem about a topic is one way to help us focus.

You might encourage your students to try writing poems about their chosen topics first to see if they can find the heart, or hearth, before they begin writing their nonfiction texts. Here's one way that writing a poem about my nonfiction topic first helped me find the focus I needed for a nonfiction text I had been working on:

For about a year, I'd been working on a picture book biography of Anne Frank. When I went to Amsterdam that summer, I visited the secret annex where Anne Frank and her family hid from the Nazis for two years. During my visit I filled my notebook with notes, impressions, and heart-wrenching facts.

Then, an editor sent out an invitation for a poetry anthology about people who have "dared to dream"—people who have inspired others with their courage, accomplishments, and perseverance. I knew immediately I wanted to write my poem about Anne Frank. But when I sat down to write, I was overcome with writer's block. There was so much in my head and heart: What would the focus of my poem be? How could I write just one poem?

As I reflected, one fact kept circling in my mind: Anne Frank and her family left their house at 7:30 in the morning on July 6, 1942, to go into hiding in the secret annex because they had been tipped off that the Nazis were going to take Anne's sister, Margo, away. I could picture the Franks leaving the house that morning. I had stood on Prinsengracht Street and could imagine them walking toward the secret annex. The heart of my poem became that moment when they left their house—the moment that, unbeknownst to them, changed not only their world forever but also ours. Anne Frank's diary would eventually become an inspiration to millions of people all around the world.

Once I found my focus, I was able to write my poem, which was published in *Dare to Dream . . . Change the World*, edited by Jill Corcoran.

This Moment

The Frank Family—Monday 7:30 A.M. July 6, 1942

Stepping over puddles on Prinsengracht Street,
shoes soaked, heavy rucksacks on their backs,
coats, caps and scarves although it's warm July;
silence between them.
Anne wonders how others on the street

can act like it's a normal day;
no knots in their stomachs, no legs trembling with fear.
At her father's office building, a spice warehouse,
they open the door—sweet cinnamon fills the air.
Now it's quiet. Office workers haven't yet arrived.
They climb the narrow staircase to the small rooms
in the back of the secret annex

where this moment turns into days
into weeks and months
into two years hiding—waiting.
Eerily ordinary days—
Westertoren church clock chiming every half hour,
playing Monopoly with Peter,
cooking supper,
eating split-pea soup and potatoes with dumplings
washing up
listening to the radio at night for news of the war
like any family.

While in hiding Anne writes to Kitty
her words thread through
her dreams;
and later
ours—
thread through every moment—
ever after.
(Heard 2013)

As you work with your students to help them find focus in their nonfiction pieces, you might share this poem, or one of your own poems or stories, before encouraging them to write poems focused on their topics.

2. Turning Facts into Scenes

Writing with Imagery

I like to view nonfiction writers as painters who transform what they see through imagery and scenes. One of my favorite genres of painting is the landscape. Landscape painters capture the physical world through light, shadow, color, and brushstrokes. Similarly, when I write nonfiction I try to communicate ideas, information, and facts by painting images with words—scenes that the reader can see in his mind, scenes that *show* rather than *tell* information.

However, not *every* fact needs to be transformed into a scene or an image. Most nonfiction writers alternately paint a scene or image to *show* information and then *tell* a fact or piece of information. A weaving of the two is a way to keep the reader's interest, as in this excerpt from *Frogs*, by Nic Bishop. Bishop states a fact and then supports it with an image of the fact:

> *Fact:* Frogs are prey, too. Birds, snakes, raccoons, and many other animals eat them.

> *Scene:* That is why many frogs are wonderfully camouflaged in colors of green or brown. When a predator wanders near, a frog will often crouch into its surroundings. It will stay very still and quiet, hoping not to be spotted. (2008, 18)

WRITING TIP
Using Imagery to Make Facts Come Alive

Have each student underline or highlight one fact from his or her research and transform the fact into a scene using imagery.

Try This

Writing with Imagery (more experienced writers)

Ask students to read the following two texts about tarantulas. Begin with the encyclopedia excerpt, and then read the second excerpt, from Jean Craighead George's book *One Day in the Desert*. Ask students to write down, or discuss with partners or the whole group, the differences they notice between the two pieces of writing.

> Tarantula is the largest of the spiders. It is named for the city of Taranto, in southern Italy, where it was first closely studied. Many tarantulas are still found there. Any of the large, hairy spiders found in large numbers in the southwestern United States and in Central America are called tarantulas. They often reach the United States in shipments of bananas. Tarantulas capture their enemies by grasping them. They live in little wells in the ground, lined and covered with silky webs. (*Encyclopedia*, s.v. "tarantula")

> Near the coyote den dwelled a tarantula, a spider almost as big as a man's fist covered with fur-like hairs. She looked like a long-legged bear, and she was sitting near the top of her burrow, a shaft she had dug straight down into the ground. The hot desert air forced her to let go with all eight legs. The spider survives the heat by digging underground and by hunting at night. The moist crickets and other insects she eats quench her thirst. (George 1996, 17)

You might want to model what you notice the difference is:

> *In the first piece of writing, there are some good facts, like the tarantula is the largest spider and tarantulas got their name from a city in southern Italy, Taranto. But in the encyclopedia excerpt there is no author's voice and you can't really picture a tarantula.*
>
> *In the second piece of writing, Jean Craighead George gives us facts about tarantulas but also shows us through description and imagery what the tarantula looks and behaves like. The author uses*

metaphor and simile to help us imagine the spider: "a spider almost as big as a man's fist covered with fur-like hairs" and "She looked like a long-legged bear."

After modeling what the difference is between the two pieces of writing, ask writers to try this independently with another topic. Students can read the examples on the reproducible (on page 59) for inspiration, or try turning factual writing (using those same examples on page 59) into scenes as the fifth graders in the following example did.

Student Example

Fifth-grade students were asked to read the following encyclopedia definition of a frog and then revise the encyclopedia version by writing new pieces on frogs, turning the encyclopedia definition's collection of facts into scenes, brought to life by imagery.

Encyclopedia Definition of Frog

Frog: a cold-blooded vertebrate animal of the class Amphibia. . . . Frogs are found all over the world, except in Antarctica. They require moisture and usually live in quiet freshwater or in the woods. Some frogs are highly aquatic, while others are better adapted to terrestrial habitats. . . . Frogs lack tails in their adult stage. They have short, neckless bodies; long, muscular hind legs specialized for jumping; and webbed feet for swimming. The skin is smooth, usually some shade of green or brown, and often spotted. Frogs have no outer ears; their prominent eardrums are exposed on the sides of the head. The bulging eyes have nictitating membranes to keep the eyes moist. Adult frogs have lungs, but their breathing mechanism is poorly developed. . . . Frogs have true voice boxes and are noted for their various sounds. Frogs capture insects and worms with their sticky, forked tongue. . . . Some large tropical species eat small mammals and snakes. A few frogs have skin glands that can produce irritating or poisonous secretions. . . . Most frogs hibernate in underwater mud and lay their eggs in early spring. (*Columbia Electronic Encyclopedia*, 6th edition, 2012, s.v. "frog")

Here is one student's revision:

Frogs

There, in the rainforest, was the cold blooded amphibian, the frog. It jumped from tree to tree then settled in its' home, on a leaf. But soon, in the spring, it would be off to lay its eggs.

Frogs live every where, except Antarctica. They can live in calm freshwater or on land. This one lives on land and swims too. Lots of frogs are green or brown. Most of the time they're spotted and smooth. Frogs are small, with no neck, webbed feet, and long, strong legs. Unlike humans they have ears that look like holes on the sides of their heads. Frogs have lungs, but their breathing is not very well developed. Frogs also have real voice boxes, so they are noticed for different sounds. Frogs help us because they trap annoying bugs with their sticky fork shaped tongues. However, frogs can be dangerous because they can carry diseases.

Try This
Writing with Imagery (less experienced writers)

For writers who are less experienced with nonfiction writing, you may want to offer more support. Instead of presenting students with a long encyclopedia passage, you may choose to start with smaller bits of factual text, encouraging students to transform them into descriptive passages. You might say something like this:

> *Sometimes nonfiction authors give the reader information by paint-ing a scene in his mind or making a movie in his mind instead of just telling the reader a fact. Chris Butterworth, who wrote* Sea Horse: The Shyest Fish in the Sea, *paints a scene by using words that give us pictures in our minds. Listen to this fact about sea horses:*
>
>> Sea horses are difficult to see in the wild—they are very still and blend in very well with their surroundings.
>
> *Now listen to how Chris Butterworth paints a scene to show us this fact. You might want to close your eyes as you listen to see what pictures come to mind:*
>
>> In the warm ocean, among the waving sea grass meadows, an eye like a small black bead is watching the fish dart by. Who does it belong to? (2006, 6)
>
> *What pictures did you see in your mind?*
> *Both the fact and the scene give us the exact same information, but Chris Butterworth's version is so much more interesting to read.*
> *Let's try one together. Let's take a fact about sea horses and write a scene that paints pictures in our readers' minds. (You can do this with the whole class, or students can try this or another fact independently.)*
>
>> Sea horses use their prehensile tail to hang out on objects such as seaweed and branching corals.

Student Examples

Here are some examples of the scenes students wrote independently:

> The waves blow wildly and the fish get tossed about. But the sea horse stays in the same place, hanging on with its tail clinging on to a piece of sea grass. —Sophia

> Fish flowing by. The sea grass just waving by. Two little eyes just peek out of the grass. —Christopher

Other Sea Horse Facts That Students Can Transform into Scenes

> Favorite sea horse habitats are coral reefs, sea grasses, and mangrove forests.

> Sea horses beat their fins very quickly, up to fifty times a second, but they do not move quickly.

> See the reproducible on page 66 for more examples of nonfiction that paints a scene.

Try This
Writing Photo-Essays: Being Inspired by Visual Imagery

Another way to encourage young writers of nonfiction to use imagery in their writing is to start with actual visual images.

For example, during my weeklong visit as a writing consultant to the American Embassy School (AES) in New Delhi, India, students were asked to write photo-essays using Lewis Hine's heartbreaking photographs of young children in the early 1900s working in textile mills and factories, found in Russell Freedman's book *Kids at Work* (1998).

Before they wrote, I gave craft minilessons on writing with imagery, precise language, and voice. One of the only rules I gave students was that the writing had to be truthful and accurate. For example, they couldn't write, "This child had only a half a bagel to eat for the entire day," if they didn't know whether a bagel was something a child would eat in the early 1900s. They could imagine and write plausible family and home situations based on their research, but whatever details they included had to be true to the historical time period and to the situation in which the children lived.

Student Examples

Students created small booklets of Lewis Hine's photos with their photo-essays, beneath which was text filled with Zinsser's ultimate criteria for quality nonfiction writing: humanity and warmth.

Through using Lewis Hine's photos, the students became impassioned in their research and advocacy for the kids who worked in factories, and they wrote vivid nonfiction pieces, full of imagery that was both historically accurate and beautifully descriptive.

In response to one of Hine's photos of a young boy, around eleven or twelve years old, standing in a factory and staring into space, Uma wrote:

> Terror and tiredness show on the faces of the young children who work countless hours everyday. Hands repeating the same motion, countless times without any breaks, "Who are these children?" some may ask but most don't because nobody wants to know the truth behind the real textile industry.

A Back-Roper in the Mule Room at Chace Cotton Mill. Burlington, Vermont

And from a Hine's photograph of a long factory room filled with thread machines, and rows of children standing by the machines, Uma again wrote:

> Clang, Clang, Clang. The noise of the machines in unison echoed through the entire building. Spools of thread soon became cloth. Meters and meters of cloth were produced. All were hunched over the machines working as fast as they could. They had to keep working. The difference between working faster and working at a normal pace could mean the difference between feeding themselves, or dying of hunger.

Another student, Lauren, created a narrative from the point of view of a child who worked in the factory:

Introduction

When children were very young, they were sent to work in factories. This photo essay shows Sophie's life from her perspective when she was a little girl. It shows what she and her friends go through every day. It explains her life, where she lives, where she eats, where she works and what she will do for the rest of her life. She will have no choices but to follow this until she dies.

One of the Spinners in Whitnel Cotton Mill

My name is Sophie. I'm not really sure how old I am or who my parents are but I have two brothers who I care a lot about but I don't see them very much because they work in the coal mines to get more money, which I can't do because I'm a girl. Which means I have to work here in a textile factory.

You can do similar work with students, particularly in history and social studies if there are pictorial records depicting important events such as the civil rights movement. Students can use photos and write accompanying photo-essays as a way to personalize history.

Turning Facts into Scenes: Writing with Imagery

Fact: Over eons of time, the peninsula of Florida was created by erosion and natural forces.

Scene: Over the eons the sea lowered, and the rock became land. The long Florida peninsula took shape in warm sunny waters.

Purple clouds, flashing with lightning, roiled and boomed above the land. Rain gushed from the storm clouds in summer. Sun bathed the land in winter. Moss grew, then ferns, then grass and trees.

The rain eroded holes in the soft limestone and filled them with water. Florida glistened with green land and blue-green lakes. (Jean Craighead George, *Everglades*, 1997)

Fact: Like most ancient cultures, the Mohawks had no formal system of writing. Their history and traditions were passed down from generation to generation through the spoken word.

Scene: During the winter months, as storms raged outside, the village storyteller would gather the children around the warmth of the longhouse fire and, accompanied by the crackling, sputtering flames and the flickering shadows, entertain them with exciting tales of their ancestors. The children sat entranced as the storyteller's voice went from a whisper to shouts and cries. With flailing arms and great leaps, he would reenact battles of men and gods and then, just as suddenly, drop to an almost inaudible hush again. (David Weitzman, *Skywalkers: Mohawk Ironworkers Build the City*, 2010, 5)

Fact: The only right a slave had was to work for his master. And work he did.

Scene: Every morning the slave driver blew the work horn or rang the bell; and all the slaves woke up, grabbed a hoe, and headed out to the fields. In the summertime the sun was up early and down late; and the air was hot, heavy, and full of mosquitoes. With each strike of the hoe to the ground the slaves sang to keep time with each other and help ease the hard work. (Kadir Nelson, *Heart and Soul: The Story of America and African Americans*, 2011, 18)

Fact: Sea horses are difficult to see in the wild—they are very still and blend in very well with their surroundings.

Scene: In the warm ocean, among the waving sea grass meadows, an eye like a small black bead is watching the fish dart by. Who does it belong to? (Chris Butterworth, *Sea Horse: The Shyest Fish in the Sea*, 2006, 6)

3. Leads

The Doorway into Writing

A lead is the doorway into writing. The first sentence or paragraph in any piece of writing needs to invite the reader in and capture the reader's attention. But a lead does a lot more than simply encourage the reader to read on. A strong lead can establish a tone, create a setting, and make us trust the writer's voice enough to want to keep reading.

Read what other authors say about how valuable a good lead is:

William Zinsser writes, "The most important sentence is the first one" (2006, 54).

Vivian Gornick says, "The experience, it seemed, was a large piece of territory. How was she to enter it? From what angle, and in what position? With what strategy, and toward what end?" (2001, 8).

John McPhee says the lead is a "flashlight" that shines down into the darkness of the story (Hart 2007, 48).

Don Fry writes that a lead "grabs the reader, informs the reader, and teaches the reader how to read the rest of the story."

And my favorite quote about leads is what Joan Didion (1978) says: "What's so hard about the first sentence is that you're stuck with it. Everything else is going

to flow out of that sentence. And by the time you've laid down the first *two* sentences, your options are all gone."

Here are some things a good lead can accomplish:

* hook the reader

* set the tone and mood

* establish the point of view

* make the author's presence felt

* grab the reader's interest and make her want to learn about the subject

* establish the direction writing will take

TYPES OF LEADS

When working with students on nonfiction writing, we tend to focus on these types of leads:

* question leads

* leads that describe the setting or paint a scene

* leads that make surprising or emotional statements

* leads that establish tone using a distinct voice

* leads that use dialogue

* leads that begin a narrative

This is certainly not an exhaustive list. You'll find, as you begin studying leads yourself, that oftentimes a good lead is a combination of several of these qualities. Following are descriptions of these types of leads and relevant excerpts of mentor texts.

Question lead By asking a question, the writer is involving the reader in the answer. Usually, a question

---

WRITING TIP

Types of Leads in Don Murray's Toolbox

There are many ways that a writer can open a piece of writing. Don Murray (2000, 93–94) names seventeen from his toolbox:

1. News: Tells the reader what the reader needs to know in the order the reader needs to know it: who, what, when, where, why.

2. Leads That Tell an Anecdote: A brief story that reveals the essence of your subject.

3. Quotation Lead: A quote lead can give additional authority and a fresh voice to the text.

4. Descriptive Lead: Sets the scene for a text.

5. Voice Lead: Voice establishes the tone of the text.

6. Announcement Lead: Tells the reader what you're going to say.

7. Tension Lead: Reveals the forces in the text and sets them in motion.

8. Problem Lead: Establishes the problem that will be solved in the text.

9. Background Lead: Provides the background so that the reader will understand the importance of the text.

10. Historical Lead: Places the story in a historical context.

11. Narrative Lead: Establishes the story as the form of the text.

12. Question Lead: Asks a question of the reader and therefore involves the reader in the fundamental issue of the story.

13. Point of View Lead: Establishes the position from which the reader will be shown the subject.

14. Reader Identification Lead: Shows readers how the story relates to them.

15. Face Lead: Gives the reader a person with whom to identify during the reading of the story.

16. Scene Lead: Sets up an action between participants in the story that reveals the central meaning of the text.

17. Dialogue Lead: Allows the story's meaning to come from the interaction of principal people in the story.

lead can't be answered by a simple yes or no. The entire text is the answer to the question, such as in this lead:

> Ever dreamed of exploring the ocean for a shipwreck? Imagine how exciting it would be to discover a hidden treasure.
>
> Think that kind of thing only happens in the movies? In 1985, Robert Ballard led a team that discovered a sunken ship called *R.M.S. Titanic*. (Stewart 2012, 5)

Lead that paints a scene The following lead paints a scene, but the author also uses short, staccato words and phrases that give the reader a sense of urgency and action and the date gives the scene a historical context:

> July 1999. One woman stands alone, off to the side of the crowd. She paces back and forth—agitated, excited, impatient. (Stone 2009, 1)

Lead that asks a question, describes a setting, and paints a scene
Next is a lead that asks a question, paints a scene, and establishes a setting using imagery and figurative language:

> Ever visit the Capitol in Washington, DC? It's a beautiful white building made of sandstone, and it has a *big* iron dome that rises over the city like a full moon. (Nelson 2011, 9)

Lead that paints a scene and makes a surprising and emotional statement This lead uses imagery to paint a scene and makes a surprising and emotional statement:

> Eleanor's father adored his "Little Golden-Hair."
> They talked.
> She danced for him.
> He hugged her and threw her into the air.
> He made her feel important and loved.
> But he drank a lot and wasn't home much.
> (Rappaport 2009, 2)

Lead that establishes tone using a distinct voice A lead can establish a tone by using a distinctive voice that impels the reader to read on:

> Seems like we've been playing baseball for a mighty long time. At least as long as we've been free. (Nelson 2008, 1)

Lead that uses dialogue Opening a piece with dialogue can hook the reader:

> "Dad, I've found a fossil."
>
> Nine-year old Matthew Berger was fossil hunting with his dad when he stumbled and spied a brown rock with a thin yellow bone stuck in it. Matthew was lucky. His father is Professor Lee Berger, a scientist who has devoted his life to finding the remains of our ancient ancestors. (Aronson 2012, 7)

Lead that begins a narrative Some leads can begin a narrative:

> One summer evening in the meadow, Oscar heard a new sound. He looked around to see who was making it. (Waring 2009)

WRITING TIP

Trying Out Different Leads

When students write nonfiction, ask them to write three different types of leads (from the types of leads above) and then decide which lead works best.

Try This Learning from Leads

Ask your nonfiction writers to read and study the leads from mentor texts that are collected into a reproducible on page 66 (or another collection of leads relevant to the work you are doing together). Students may do this work either collaboratively or independently.

You might ask students to consider these questions as they read and discuss the leads:

Questions to Think About as You Read Leads

✦ What type of lead is the author using?

✦ Does the lead hook you? If yes, how does it do this?

✦ What is the nonfiction genre (narrative nonfiction, biography, autobiography, informational text, feature article, etc.)? How can you tell from the lead?

✦ What do you learn about the topic from the lead?

✦ What is the tone or point of view of the lead?

✦ Can you tell from the lead what the rest of the book will be about?

After they have read, studied, and (if they are working in partnerships or small groups) discussed some examples, you might use the following questions to guide a class conversation about effective leads in nonfiction writing:

✦ What do you notice about the examples of leads: do they establish a tone, create a setting, set up a problem, or paint a scene?

✦ Do the leads prove that Joan Didion (1978) is right when she says: "Everything else is going to flow out of that [first] sentence. And by the time you've laid down the first two sentences, your options are all gone"?

✦ What kind of writing (point of view, descriptive, narrative, etc.) do you think will flow out of the first two sentences of the lead examples?

✦ Which lead is your favorite, and why?

Student Examples

After engaging in this kind of study and discussion, the students in one eighth-grade history class were able to liven up their nonfiction leads tremendously. The students had been researching the Roman emperor Justinian and had been asked to write research texts about him. When students started writing, the teacher noticed that the writing seemed dry and lifeless, like it had been copied from an encyclopedia. So the class took a break to study the leads from of a variety of history mentor texts. Then writers returned to their texts to rewrite *their leads only*, using Joan Didion's quote (and all that they'd learned from studying mentor texts) as inspiration.

Following is both the original and the revised lead written by one of the eighth graders:

Original Lead

The emperor Justinian was the Roman emperor of Constantinople from 526 A.D. to 565 A.D. Justinian was the protégé of his uncle, Justin, who was the Byzantine emperor from 518 A.D.. to 527 A.D. Justinian worked as the co-emperor for his uncle Justin until the day his uncle died. When Justinian's uncle died, he and his wife, Theodora, became the rulers of Constantinople.

Revised Lead

What if our modern day legal system was as bloody and barbaric as the Justinian code? A system where you could pour hot molten lead slowly into an offender's mouth, or chisel away at a hand, an eye, a tongue, etc. As a matter of fact, some of our legal system and other countries' legal systems as well were based on the Justinian code.

Not only is the revised lead much more interesting than the original, but the student's focus has changed as well. In the original, it's hard to tell what the focus is: it's simply a list of emperor Justinian's lineage. But in the revised version, the writer's focus is clear: it's on the Justinian code and emperor Justinian's influence even into modern times. Also, look at how the point of view has changed from third-person objective in the original lead, where the writer is distant, to a combination of second- and third-person points of view, where the writer directly addresses the reader. The voice of the writer in the second lead is much more present as well.

Leads

Lead That Uses Descriptive Language, Distinctive Voice

It's hours past midnight. You'd think any self-respecting parrot would be asleep. But not Lisa.

No, despite the late hour, this huge, soft, moss-green bird, looking somewhat like a parakeet who has eaten one side of the mushroom in *Alice and Wonderland* and grown into an eight-pound giant, decides this is a great time to waddle out of her nest—a nest that's not in a tree, like a normal parrot's, but *underground*. (Sy Montgomery, *Kakapo Rescue: Saving the World's Strangest Parrot*, 2010, 1)

Lead That Has Action, Paints a Scene, Establishes a Setting, Sets Up a Problem

A Stormy Night
October 22, 1707

It was a mean and dirty night. The wind howled, and waves the size of small mountains crashed against the ship.

Suddenly there was a sickening thud. A loud crack. The ship shuddered, then split open. (Kathryn Lasky, *The Man Who Made Time Travel*, 2003, 1)

Lead That Has a Familiar Tone, Uses Everyday Language, Uses Second-Person Point of View

Most folks my age and complexion don't speak much about the past. Sometimes it's just too hard to talk about—nothing we like to share with you young folk. No parent wants to tell a child that he was once a slave and made to do another man's bidding. Or that she had to swallow her pride and take what she was given, even though she knew it wasn't fair. Our story is chock-full of things like this. Things that might make you cringe, or feel angry. But there are also parts that will make you proud, or even laugh a little. You gotta take the good with the bad, I guess. You have to know where you come from so you can move forward. (Kadir Nelson, *Heart and Soul: The Story of America and African Americans*, 2011, prologue)

Lead That Establishes a Setting and a Historical Context, Creates Suspense

On the morning of July 2, 1937, the coast guard cutter *Itasca* drifted on the Pacific Ocean, waiting . . . listening. . . .

Hundreds of miles to the west, the famous female pilot Amelia Earhart was winging her way toward Howland Island—a narrow spit of coral sand just to the west of the ship. (Candace Fleming, *Amelia Lost: The Life and Disappearance of Amelia Earhart*, 2011, 1)

Lead That Uses Descriptive Language, Paints a Scene

The Mysterious Creature

Before dawn, the giant creature is almost invisible. It sits in shadow in its rocky, horseshoe-shaped hollow. Then, as the sun slowly rises in the east, the creature's body is gradually revealed. . . . (James Cross Giblin, *Secrets of the Sphinx*, 2004, 4)

Lead That Establishes a Setting and a Historical Context, Creates a Scene, Asks a Question

Chapter One: A Grave Mystery

On August 16, 2005, the air temperature on the bank of the James River in Jamestown, Virginia, hovered at 100°F (38°C). Sunlight flooded the beige-colored soil. At the bottom of a carefully excavated pit, the rounded surface of a human skull gleamed with a yellow brown luster. The teeth shone white against the darker jawbone and brownish soil beneath. The skeleton's leg bones stretched long and straight, toward the end of the grave. In contrast, the arms were chaotically bent. The left arm lay across the body, with the right flung up toward the shoulder.

Who was this person? (Sally M. Walker, *Written in Bone: Buried Lives of Jamestown and Colonial Maryland*, 2009, 8)

4. Point of View and Voice

Who Are We When We Write?

Who is speaking when we write nonfiction? What is our relationship to our audience? What view of the world are we showing our readers? What lens do we use as we write? What do we allow the reader to see and hear?

Voice and point of view are two threads woven together to make a whole cloth. Although they are closely related, they are not the same. Point of view is the lens the writer gives to the reader through which to view the material, and voice is the identity of the writer.

POINT OF VIEW

Constance Hale (2010) writes, "In writing, the connection between storyteller and audience is just as important. By using some subtle devices, a narrator can reach out to the reader and say, 'We're in this together.'"

The subtle device that Hale refers to is the writer's point of view. Here are four points of view from which you can choose to write: first person; second person; third-person objective; and third-person omniscient.

First person When an author writes in the first person, he uses words like *I*, *we, me, us, my,* or *mine*. The writer is putting himself into the writing. The tone is personal, and the writer becomes a character in the piece. The first-person point of view draws readers into the writing by showing us what the writer is experiencing, observing, thinking, or feeling. The disadvantage of using the first person is that the writer is limited to a single point of view, unlike when writing in the third person.

Personal and persuasive essays, opinion pieces, memoirs and autobiographies, book reviews, travel writing, and some informational texts are written in the first person.

Second person Writing in the second person uses the pronouns *you* and *yours* to address the reader directly. The second-person point of view is compelling because readers feel an immediate connection to the writer, as she is speaking directly to us.

Informational texts, personal and persuasive essays, opinion pieces, and even autobiographies can be written in the second person.

Third-person objective The third-person objective uses the pronouns *he* and *she*. This point of view describes things as they are seen from the outside and does not have access to anyone's thoughts, like the third-person omniscient does. The writer is not present except for in the tone of the piece.

Informational texts, biography, historical narrative, and journalism can be written in the third-person objective.

Third-person omniscient With the third-person omniscient point of view, the voice of the writer knows everything there is to know—kind of an "all-seeing eye." The writer can even enter the minds of his subjects when writing in third-person omniscient.

Historical narrative, journalism, and biographies can be written in the third-person omniscient.

Point of view is the lens the writer gives to the reader through which to view the material, and voice is the identity of the writer.

Try This Studying Point of View

Ask your nonfiction writers to read and study the point-of-view examples on the repro-ducible on page 71 (or another collection of point-of-view mentor texts that you choose).

As students read the excerpts collaboratively or independently, ask them to think about these questions:

+ Do you hear the difference in the tone and voice of each one?

+ Which point of view draws the reader in close?

+ Who are the different audiences for which these nonfiction pieces are written?

+ If you substituted another point of view, how would it change the writing?

+ What subgenres (informative/explanatory, autobiography, opinion, and so on) do these nonfiction pieces belong to? Does it make sense that a particular subgenre should be written in a certain point of view?

As your students craft their own nonfiction writing, ask them to carefully consider the point of view they are choosing to write in, and to evaluate how that point of view af-fects the way the text will be read. You may even encourage students to try writing about the same topic using a few different points of view to determine which is the best fit.

Point of View

First-Person Point of View

I drive south from my home in central California to San Diego. There I spend several days helping load scientific equipment aboard the NOAA ship *McArthur II* and setting up our work areas. Over the flying bridge, the highest deck on the ship, the ship's crew has strung a canvas canopy to provide shade. We will be grateful for the shade as we head south into the sunny tropics. (Sophie Webb, *Far from Shore: Chronicles of an Open Ocean Voyage*, 2011, 6)

It is a typical September day in western England—we had heavy rain yesterday, and the sky is still slate gray, but when the clouds break there are sudden moments of clear sunlight. I keep noticing the changing light because I am dashing to stay out of the way of a Japanese film crew. They are following the archeologist Mike Parker Pearson as he leads them around Stonehenge—the mysterious circle of stones that was built on Salisbury Plain 4,500 years ago and is now a World Heritage site. (Marc Aronson, *If Stones Could Speak: Unlocking the Secrets of Stonehenge*, 2010, 7)

Second-Person Point of View

Imagine a long time ago, in your family.

Do you remember old photographs of your great-grandparents? Perhaps you have seen an ancestor's portrait that was painted even before photography was invented. (Lawrence Pringle, *Billions of Years, Amazing Changes: The Story of Evolution*, 2011, 11)

You're swimming in the warm blue sea. What's the one word that turns your dream into a nightmare? (Nicola Davies, *Surprising Sharks*, 2003, 6)

Third-Person Point of View

One cold winter morning, just off the east coast of Florida, a baby female dolphin managed to get tangled up in a crab trap. In an effort to free herself, the dolphin caused the ropes securing the crab trap to the buoy to become wrapped around her tail. (Juliana Hatkoff, Isabella Hatkoff, and Craig Hatkoff, *Winter's Tail: How One Little Dolphin Learned to Swim Again*, 2011, 1)

Third-Person Omniscient Point of View

Nine-year-old Peter Zimmerman searched the sky for airplanes. It was 1948, and Peter stood in his uncle's yard in West Berlin, Germany. There had been a time, three or four years earlier, when the droning of American and British bombers would have sent Peter running for cover. But World War II was over, and things had changed. *Now the aircraft didn't frighten him.* In fact, *he longed to see a particular American plane*—one that would fly over and wiggle its wings. (Michael O. Tunnell, *Candy Bomber: The Story of the Berlin Airlift's "Chocolate Pilot,"* 2010, 1; emphasis added)

Combination: First, Second, and Third

Most folks my age and complexion don't speak much about the past. Sometimes it's just too hard to talk about—nothing we like to share with you young folk. No parent wants to tell a child that he was once a slave and made to do another man's bidding. Or that she had to swallow her pride and take what she was given, even though she knew it wasn't fair. Our story is chock-full of things like this. Things that might make you cringe, or feel angry. But there are also parts that will make you proud, or even laugh a little. You gotta take the good with the bad, I guess. You have to know where you come from so you can move forward. (Kadir Nelson, *Heart and Soul: The Story of America and African Americans*, 2011, 7)

VOICE: WHO ARE WE WHEN WE WRITE?

Voice is difficult to teach because it's so subtle and can be reflected in many different ways, including diction, word choice, sentence patterns, and tone.

The audience and purpose of a piece can also influence voice. Here are several questions to think about when considering the voice of a mentor text:

* What kinds of words does the writer use: slang, vernacular, everyday, or poetic?

* How does the choice of words reflect the writer's voice?

* Is the writer's voice formal or familiar?

* Is the writer's voice conversational?

* What is the attitude or tone of the writer?

* Is the writer's voice authoritative or relaxed?

* Is the writer's voice distant or personal?

As students become more familiar with nonfiction, they can begin to notice an author's voice as distinct from point of view. Once they begin to identify nonfiction mentor texts, they can ask themselves what kind of voice they are drawn to. As they begin to write their own nonfiction, they can ask what kind of voice they want to convey to their audience: Familiar or formal? Personal or professional? Students may want to try on several different voices as they write; for example, one voice can be personal as if talking to a close friend, and another voice can be a little more formal as if teaching a large class. They can then decide which voice is more appropriate for their audience.

The audience and purpose of a piece can also influence voice.

Try This   Considering Voice

Read the three voice mentor texts from the reproducible on page 75. Each of these excerpts is from a nonfiction text about one man—Abraham Lincoln—but the voice of each piece is distinct. This exercise asks students to study the mentor texts and to notice and describe their differences.

As writers read independently or listen to you read aloud the three voice mentor texts, you might ask them to consider and discuss the questions listed on page 73 about each author's voice.

Students can then try on three different voices as they begin to write, using the mentor texts about Abraham Lincoln as inspiration.

Voice: Who Are We When We Write?

These three mentor texts are all about Abraham Lincoln:

One day while walking through the park on my way to breakfast I saw a very tall man. He reminded me of someone, but I could not think who.

At the coffee shop I ordered pancakes. They were DELICIOUS.

We paid with a Lincoln and two Washingtons. And then I remembered. The man I had seen looked exactly like Abraham Lincoln. (Maira Kalman, *Looking at Lincoln*, 2012)

Deep in the wilderness down in Kentucky there stood a cabin of roughly hewn logs. It was a poor little cabin of only one room. The February wind tore at the clumsy door and made it rattle on its leather hinges. Just a glimmer of daylight sifted in through the oiled deer hide stretched across the single window frame. But flames flickered gaily on the hearth. In this cabin lived a man named Thomas Lincoln with his wife and his little daughter, Sally. And here it was that his son, Abraham Lincoln, first saw the world on a Sunday morning. (Ingri and Edgar Parin D'Aulaire, *Abraham Lincoln*, 2008)

There are 365 birthdays, one for every day of the year, and I have the same one as Abraham Lincoln. February 12th. A day of winter when we both were born.

When February comes, we talk about Abraham Lincoln in class. My teacher, Mrs. Giff, hangs 28 pictures of Lincoln along the hall. (Louise Borden, *A. Lincoln and Me*, 2009)

5. Precise Language

Details, Details, and More Details

Details and precise language are at the core of nonfiction writing. All writers use details to support a topic or theme, but choosing meaningful details makes the difference between writing that springs to life and writing that is flat and uninteresting. William Strunk Jr. and E. B. White write in *Elements of Style*, "The surest way to arouse and hold the reader is to be specific, definite, and concrete. . . . The greatest writers . . . are effective largely because they deal in particulars and report the details that matter" (1999, 21).

But for many young writers, the idea of using details is frustrating. Simply telling students, "I think you need to add details," doesn't help them to discover what *kinds* of details will make their nonfiction texts stronger and more engaging.

A nonfiction writer's process of gathering research will guide her in including relevant details. Science writer Nic Bishop researches animals using firsthand observation through photography, which gives him a chance to look closely at the animals he writes about and then translate those details into writing. In the following example, I can picture Nic Bishop silently observing the frog, camera in hand: "When an animal comes by, the frog watches attentively, waiting until it moves closer. Then it seizes the prey with a loud snap of its huge mouth" (2008, 17).

Washington Post journalist DeNeen L. Brown said the following about using details in researching for newspaper articles: "The colors, the smell, the marked-up pages of his Bible. . . . Oftentimes, when I'm in these situations interviewing people, I have a finite amount of time. As they're speaking and the tape recorder is rolling, I'm writing down these details all the time. It's like, what am I struck by? Her kitchen is perfectly clean. It's black and white. A little girl sitting in her high chair, but she's not eating her Cheerios, all the things that are happening around me" (Scanlan 1999).

But it's important to remember that too many details can overpower the writing if they are not chosen wisely. Selecting those details that best support the focus of the text is essential.

Details can be many things, including

* sensory words

* precise language: concrete and precise nouns and verbs

* figurative language

* domain-specific vocabulary

> *But it's important to remember that too many details can overpower the writing if they are not chosen wisely.*

SENSORY WORDS

The doorway into a writer's experience is through the physical world. Nonfiction writers use sensory and descriptive words that can make the reader see, touch, hear, smell, and even taste.

No matter what the subgenre, a nonfiction writer's goal is to help the reader experience what he is describing. Rick Bragg, a journalist for the *New York Times*, gives this advice to young writers: "I tell people to always be looking. I know that sounds a little absurd, but you just keep your eyes open, soak in how something smells or tastes or sounds" (Scanlan 1996).

Another journalist, DeNeen L. Brown, gives similar advice: "When I sit down to write a story, I want people to see the story, I want people to feel what I feel, hear what I hear, taste what I taste, smell what I smell" (Scanlan 1999).

Try This Using Sensory Words

Read the sensory language mentor texts on page 79 aloud to your students and ask them to listen for any sensory description and to name which senses each writer is highlighting. Then reread those parts and try to identify which sensory words make the writing come alive. Write favorite sensory words on index cards and display them around the room to inspire students as they write, or have them keep lists of sensory words in their writing notebooks.

You can give a minilesson on "cracking open" words, phrases, and sentences in nonfiction writing by revising and adding sensory language. In a minilesson on revising for sensory language, I often compare and contrast what an author could have written and what an author actually wrote. For example, in *The Watcher: Jane Goodall's Life with the Chimps*, Jeanette Winter (2011) could have written: "That first night, Jane lay awake listening to *new sounds* and looking up at the stars. She knew she was Home." But instead she cracked open *new sounds* and described the sounds using sensory language: "—the croak of a frog, the hum of crickets, the laugh of a hyena, the hoot of an owl—." Students can read their nonfiction writing and look for places where they could add sensory words.

Sensory Words

That first night, Jane lay awake listening to new sounds—*the croak of a frog, the hum of crickets, the laugh of a hyena, the hoot of an owl*—and looking up at the stars. She knew she was Home. (Jeanette Winter, *The Watcher: Jane Goodall's Life with the Chimps*, 2011; emphasis added)

It is a typical September day in western England—we had heavy rain yesterday, and *the sky is still slate gray, but when the clouds break there are sudden moments of clear sunlight.* (Marc Aronson, *If Stones Could Speak: Unlocking the Secrets of Stonehenge*, 2010, 7; emphasis added)

> I **see** the ocean,
> gray, green, blue. . . .
>
> I **hear** the ocean,
> a lion's roar,
> crashing rumors
> toward the shore, . . .
>
> I **touch** the ocean,
> and the surf gives chase, . . .
> (Pam Muñoz Ryan, *Hello Ocean*, 2001)

Precise Language: Concrete Nouns and Active Verbs

Strong, active verbs and concrete nouns are what make a nonfiction sentence effective. Many people believe that the more adjectives a writer uses, the more descriptive the writing is. Actually, the active verbs and the concrete nouns are what make nonfiction writing come alive. Verbs are the engines of a sentence and give it energy. Concrete nouns are the wheels on which the sentence revolves.

Look at the following example from *A Seed Is Sleepy*, by Dianna Hutts Aston.

> To find a spot to grow, a seed might *leap* from its pod, or
> *cling* to a child's shoestring, or *tumble* through a bear's
> belly. (2007; emphasis added)

The verbs in this sentence are surprising and precise. Imagine if Dianna Hutts Aston had used vague verbs instead, like in this revised version: "a seed might *be in* its pod, or *be on* a child's shoestring, or *be in* a bear's belly." Without the active verbs, the sentence has lost its vitality.

Concrete nouns like *tree*, *desk*, *river*, and *cloud* name people, places, and things that we can see and feel, and build pictures in our minds. It's the well-chosen concrete noun that makes the difference. Why choose *flower* when the options include *rose*, *tulip*, *peony*, and *daffodil*? In contrast, abstract nouns like *devotion*, *beauty*, *love*, *glory*, and *time* name things that we cannot physically see, hear, smell, taste, or feel. They describe qualities and are difficult to picture. They describe qualities and identify concepts, experiences, ideas, qualities, and feeling but are difficult to picture.

Although I encourage students to try to use mostly precise and concrete nouns when writing nonfiction, sometimes abstract nouns do serve an important purpose as they can express large ideas, emotion, beliefs, or a writer's state of being, which is necessary in some nonfiction writing.

If we go back to Dianna Hutts Aston and change her concrete nouns to vague and abstract nouns, let's see what happens to the power of the sentence:

> To find a spot to grow, a seed might leap from *where it
> grew*, or cling to *something*, or tumble through *an animal*.

Without those magnificent concrete nouns—*pod*; *child's shoestring*; and *bear's belly*—the sentence has also lost its vitality.

Strong, active verbs and concrete nouns are what make a nonfiction sentence effective.

Many writers make the mistake of writing description using as many juicy adjectives as they can. Ironically, it's the concrete nouns that supplement the adjectives and lessen the need for them.

Let's look at the description that follows. Most people might think that this excerpt contains more adjectives than any other parts of speech. Not true. It's the concrete nouns and action-packed verbs that really give this writing impact. In fact, in my count there are seventeen concrete nouns, nine active verbs, and just five adjectives.

> Sunbeams fall in slender shafts through a canopy of swamp maples. The water is dappled in a confetti of pale light. Dewdrops sparkle on the reeds.
>
> A warm breeze ripples over the water and awakens the insects along the shore. Water striders stand on delicate legs, skating the surface in short pulses. Below them, whirligig beetles tumble and dive in the shallows like a troupe of acrobats. It is not safe here. (Heinz 2005)

Many writers make the mistake of writing description using as many juicy adjectives as they can.

For a fun and informative exercise for students, send them off with a non-fiction passage—either the one above or one you've chosen for its vivid, precise language. Ask them to read the excerpt once and guess whether there are more concrete nouns, active verbs, or adjectives. Then have them count and tally. Gather the students together to discuss what they've noticed and what it means for their own writing.

Avoid Weak Words and Construction

Linguistic studies show that English speakers can better remember writing that uses an active voice rather than a passive voice because it's more concrete and less wordy than the passive voice. So if your students want to engage their readers, they should transform their writing into the active voice. In the passive voice, the object of the action is the subject of the sentence; that is, the subject is being acted upon by something else, often not named in the sentence. For example, "We were driven to the game" (passive) versus "Our mother drove us to the game" (active). So the passive voice is definitely less desirable because it can be more vague and indirect since the true subjects (the actors) are sometimes left out.

Avoid Overuse of the Verb *to Be*

The verb *to be* is the most commonly used verb in the English language. It comes in many forms depending on case or tense, such as *am, is, are, was, were*. The problem with using *to be* too much is that it can make writing dull. Students can instead substitute stronger, more vivid verbs to strengthen writing.

> *Examples of Abstract and Vague Nouns to Avoid*
>
> things
> stuff
> beauty
> niceness
> glory
> devotion

And writers should use the following imprecise words sparingly: *very, all, important, seem, often, big, small, have, got.*

Try This   Using Precise Language

After a class conversation about concrete nouns and active verbs, send students off to read the mentor texts appearing on the reproducible on page 84. Ask them to identify the concrete nouns and active verbs in each excerpt by highlighting or underlining them. You may ask students to then brainstorm a few alternative concrete nouns and active verbs that would work in these pieces.

As students work on their own nonfiction pieces, you might ask them to scan their pieces with an eye out for abstract nouns, passive construction, or weak verbs. Once they've identified some, they can revise by substituting concrete nouns and active verbs. They might work in pairs, discussing together how making the language more precise brings their nonfiction writing to life.

Precise Language: Concrete Nouns and Active Verbs

Active Verbs

As it *hops* down the bark, it *nips* and *nabs* beetles, ants and other insects and their eggs, as well as caterpillars, spiders and flies. (Mel Boring, *Birds, Nests and Eggs*, 1998, 32; emphasis added)

So the hatchlings wait until night. Then they *burst* through the sand and *skitter* toward the sea. (Nicola Davies, *One Tiny Turtle*, 2001b, 26; emphasis added)

At the bottom of a carefully excavated pit, the rounded surface of a human skull *gleamed* with a yellow brown luster. The teeth *shone* white against the darker jawbone and the brownish soil beneath. (Sally M. Walker, *Written in Bone: Buried Lives of Jamestown and Colonial Maryland*, 2009, 8; emphasis added)

Concrete Nouns

On the *morning* of July 2, 1937, the *coast guard cutter Itasca* drifted on the *Pacific Ocean*, waiting . . . listening. . . . (Candace Fleming, *Amelia Lost: The Life and Disappearance of Amelia Earhart*, 2011, 1; emphasis added)

One cold winter morning, just off the *east coast* of *Florida*, a *baby female dolphin* managed to get tangled up in a *crab trap*. (Juliana Hatkoff, Isabella Hatkoff, and Craig Hatkoff, *Winter's Tail: How One Little Dolphin Learned to Swim Again*, 2011, 1; emphasis added)

Sensory Adjectives

. . . *damp stretchy* skin . . . (Nic Bishop, *Frogs*, 2008, 5; emphasis added)

The blue whale eats krill—*pale pinkish shrimplike* creatures the size of your little finger. (Nicola Davies, *Big Blue Whale*, 1997, 14; emphasis added)

FIGURATIVE LANGUAGE

I once heard a lecture given by the nonfiction writer Seymour Simon. He spoke in a large ballroom at a conference hotel. He was speaking about outer space and how the human mind has a difficult time understanding the vastness of the universe and our solar system. To help us comprehend just how gigantic Jupiter is compared with Earth, he asked us to each put a hand in the air and make a fist. He told us that if Earth were the size of our fist, Jupiter, in comparison, would be the size of the ballroom we were sitting in. He was making a metaphor of sorts—a concrete comparison that helped us comprehend just how large Jupiter was. We all grasped the concrete metaphor immediately.

Nonfiction writers use figurative language, such as metaphor and simile, as frequently as poets do. Figurative language is a way for nonfiction writers to be precise, to help the reader visualize, and to help writing come alive.

Here are a few examples from mentor texts:

> West Berliners were excited to see *the steady stream of great silver birds* crowding their sky. (Tunnell 2010, 2; emphasis added)

> Ever visit the Capitol in Washington, DC? It's a beautiful white building made of sandstone, and it has a *big iron dome that rises over the city like a full moon*. (Nelson 2011, 9; emphasis added)

> Now she unhooks her toes and drops into black space. *With a sound like a tiny umbrella opening*, she flaps her wings. (Davies 2001a, 8; emphasis added)

Figurative language is a way for nonfiction writers to be precise, to help the reader visualize, and to help writing come alive.

These are a few examples from student writers using similes to transform a fact about sea horses:

> A sea horse wraps its tale around a waving blade of sea-
> weed. It's like a water possum in sky blue water. —Logan

A see horse wraps his tale around a waving blade of sea weed he's like a water posom in sky blue water.

> A sea horse uses its tail to hang onto things like a leaf
> hanging from a tree and the deep blue water swaying all
> around. —Alexander

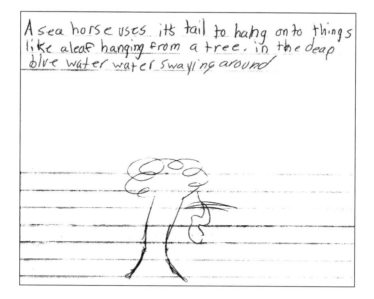

A sea horse uses its tail to hang on to things like a leaf hanging from a tree. in the deap blue water water swayling around

A sea horse puts its tail and hooks it onto a piece of coral like someone sewing two pieces of cloth together.
—Caroline

Scene: A Seahorse puts its tail and hooks it onto a piece of coral like someone sewing two pieces of cloth together.

Students can study more figurative language mentor texts in the reproducibles on pages 89 and 90, discuss the kinds of figurative language authors use and why, and then write their own examples of figurative language in nonfiction texts they are already working on.

In addition to metaphor and simile, nonfiction writers use other types of figurative language, such as *personification*, which is when writers give human qualities to an inanimate object, plant, or animal. One of my favorite nonfiction books is *A Seed Is Sleepy*, by Dianna Hutts Aston (2007). Instead of just telling us facts about seeds, she personifies them, and helps the reader visualize information about seeds:

> A seed is *sleepy*.
>   It *lies* there, *tucked* inside its flowers on its cone, or beneath the soil. *Snug. Still.* (emphasis added)

Try This

Using Personification to Make Nonfiction Writing Come Alive

After you've discussed the idea of personification with your students, you might write the following excerpt from *A Seed Is Sleepy* (Aston 2007) on chart paper so that all students are able to read it. Ask them to either explain to a partner or write down what *information* the author is trying to get across when she writes:

> A seed is sleepy.
> It lies there, tucked inside its flowers on its cone, or beneath the soil.
> Snug. Still.
>
> A seed is secretive.
> It does not reveal itself too quickly.

Ask students to discuss how personification helps Aston get the information across in a lively, engaging way. You might then ask students to write another sentence or two about seeds using personification. First, they might brainstorm some characteristics of seeds, and then they could transform these facts using personification (similar to how students transformed facts about sea horses into scenes on page 56). For example:

Facts About Seeds

✦ Seeds travel.

✦ Seeds form roots underground.

✦ Seeds grow upward toward sunlight.

If students need support, you might give them an example of your own, like "Milkweed seeds zoom across the meadow wearing little white skirts."

If your students need other models from the text, you might read the rest of *A Seed Is Sleepy* and see other ways Dianna Hutts Aston personifies seeds, or read the other examples on the reproducible on page 90.

After they've had a chance to practice with seed facts, suggest that students try using personification in the context of their own nonfiction pieces.

Figurative Language: Simile and Metaphor

But Henry's mother knew things could change. "Do you see those leaves blowing in the wind? They are torn from the trees *like slave children are torn from their families*." (Ellen Levine, *Henry's Freedom Box: A True Story from the Underground Railroad*, 2007; emphasis added)

Daisy was a small woman, but *she had the force of a hurricane*, and her family and friends knew from experience that *she would stir up their daily lives* in delightful, unpredictable, and sometimes exasperating ways whenever she returned home. So, everyone would learn that Daisy planned to launch the Girl Guides movement in Savannah. But this time, *the "hurricane" intended to shake up not just her hometown but the entire country*. (Ginger Wadsworth, *First Girl Scout: The Life of Juliette Gordon*, 2012, xiii; emphasis added)

Reach out and touch the blue whale's skin. It's *springy and smooth like a hard-boiled egg*, and it's as *slippery as wet soap*. Look into its eye. It's as *big as a teacup* and as *dark as the deep sea*. Just behind the eye is *a hole as small as the end of a pencil*. (Nicola Davies, *Big Blue Whale*, 1997, 9; emphasis added)

Figurative Language: Personification

A seed is *sleepy.*

    It *lies* there, *tucked* inside its flowers on its cone, or beneath the soil. *Snug. Still.*

    A seed is *secretive.*

    It does not *reveal itself too quickly.* (Dianna Hutts Aston, *A Seed Is Sleepy*, 2007; emphasis added)

Hummingbird

Ruby-throated hummingbird

zig-

       zags

                      from morning glories

to honeysuckle

     sipping

honey

                 from a straw

all day long.

(Georgia Heard, *Creatures of Earth, Sea and Sky: Animal Poems*, 1992, 7; emphasis added)

Far, far out to sea . . .

empty sky *touches* the water.

(Nicola Davies, *One Tiny Turtle*, 2001b, 6; emphasis added)

Babysitting Bugs

When most insects lay eggs, they leave them alone. This female parent bug is different. (Sue Malyan, *Bugs: A Close-Up Look at Insects and Their Relatives*, 2005, 18; emphasis added)

DOMAIN-SPECIFIC VOCABULARY

Most of us know that a group of fish is called a *school* of fish but not every animal group is called a school; the word for a group changes when we're writing about different animals, such as a *troop* of baboons, an *army* of caterpillars, a *herd* of cattle or cranes, and—the strangest and most surprising word—a *murder* of crows. If I were reading a nonfiction text on crows and the writer wrote "a group of crows" instead of "a murder of crows," I'd know that the writer had not done her research on crows.

These specific words are called *domain-specific vocabulary*. A nonfiction writer needs to be informed enough about his topic to include the vocabulary that is specific to it.

When Nicola Davies writes in *Bat Loves the Night* about where bats sleep, she doesn't just say that bats sleep in beds; she writes instead, "The place where bats sleep in the day is called a *roost*. It can be a building, a cave, or a tree, so long as it's dry and safe" (2001a, 20; emphasis added). She is introducing readers to a domain-specific word.

And when Gail Gibbons writes about lighthouses in *Beacons of Light: Lighthouses*, she uses a domain-specific word: "The *diaphone*, one of the best foghorns, uses compressed air to give off two tones, a high pitched screech and a low grunt" (1990; emphasis added).

Nonfiction writers weave domain-specific words into writing to help define, be precise, and give the reader specific information about a topic.

> ### WRITING TIP
> **Gathering Domain-Specific Vocabulary**
>
> As students are researching topics, ask them to reserve a page in their notes to generate a list of domain-specific words related to their topics so that that they can weave them into the main body of their texts.

LINKS TO THE COMMON CORE STATE STANDARDS: PRECISE LANGUAGE

English Language Arts Standards: Writing

All emphasis added.

Text Types and Purposes
3–5

CCSS.ELA-Literacy.W.3.2: Write **informative/explanatory texts** to examine a topic and convey ideas and information clearly.

> **CCSS.ELA-Literacy.W.3.2b:** Develop the topic with facts, definitions, and *details*.

> **CCSS.ELA-Literacy.W.4.2b, 5.2b:** Develop the topic with facts, definitions, *concrete details*, quotations, or other information and examples related to the topic.

> **CCSS.ELA-Literacy.W.4.2d, 5.2d:** Use *precise language* and *domain-specific vocabulary* to inform about or explain the topic.

6–8

CCSS.ELA-Literacy.W.6.2, 7.2, 8.2: Write **informative/explanatory texts** to examine a topic and convey ideas, concepts, and information through the selection, organization, and analysis of relevant content.

> **CCSS.ELA-Literacy.W.6.2b, 7.2b:** Develop the topic with relevant facts, definitions, *concrete details*, quotations, or other information and examples.

> **CCSS.ELA-Literacy.W.8.2b:** Develop the topic with relevant, well-chosen facts, definitions, *concrete details*, quotations, or other information and examples.

> **CCSS.ELA-Literacy.W.6.2d, 7.2d, 8.2d:** Use *precise language* and *domain-specific vocabulary* to inform about or explain the topic.

3–5

CCSS.ELA-Literacy.W.3.3: Write **narratives** to develop real or imagined experiences or events using effective technique, *descriptive details*, and clear event sequences.

> **CCSS.ELA-Literacy.W.3.3b:** Use dialogue and *descriptions* of actions, thoughts, and feelings to develop experiences and events or show the response of characters to situations.

> **CCSS.ELA-Literacy.W.4.3b:** Use dialogue and *description* to develop experiences and events or show the responses of characters to situations.

> **CCSS.ELA-Literacy.W.5.3b:** Use narrative techniques, such as dialogue, *description*, and pacing, to develop experiences and events or show the responses of characters to situations.

> **CCSS.ELA-Literacy.W.4.3d, 5.3d:** Use *concrete words and phrases* and *sensory details* to convey experiences and events precisely.

6–8

CCSS.ELA-Literacy.W.6.3, 7.3, 8.3: Write **narratives** to develop real or imagined experiences or events using effective technique, *relevant descriptive details*, and well-structured event sequences.

> **CCSS.ELA-Literacy.W.6.3b, 7.3b, 8.3b:** Use narrative techniques, such as dialogue, pacing, *description*, and reflection, to develop experiences, events, and/or characters.

> **CCSS.ELA-Literacy.W.6.3d, 7.3d, 8.3d:** Use *precise words and phrases*, relevant *descriptive details*, and *sensory language* to capture the action and convey experiences and events.

Literacy in History/Social Studies, Science, and Technical Subjects

CCSS.ELA-Literacy.WHST.6–8.2: Write **informative/explanatory texts**, including the narration of historical events, scientific procedures/experiments, or technical processes.

> **CCSS.ELA-Literacy.WHST.6–8.2b:** Develop the topic with relevant, well-chosen facts, definitions, *concrete details*, quotations, or other information and examples.

> **CCSS.ELA-Literacy.WHST.6–8.2d:** Use *precise language* and *domain-specific vocabulary* to inform about or explain the topic.

Try This Generating Domain-Specific Vocabulary

Think of a topic together as a class. Generate as many domain-specific words as you can for that topic. A good place to find domain-specific vocabulary is in the glossary in the back of a nonfiction book, which lists and defines words that the reader might not know, most often including examples of domain-specific vocabulary. Keep in mind that not every word in a glossary is a domain-specific word; a glossary can also include other words that might be unknown to the reader.

You might begin by showing students what a glossary looks like, if they are unfamiliar with this text feature. Write some of the domain-specific words found in the glossary on chart paper, and then work together to find those words in the main body of the text.

Here are a few examples of domain-specific words about bats that appear in the text and the glossary of *Owls, Bats, Wolves and Other Nocturnal Animals* (Hirschmann 2003, 32):

Colony—a group of bats that live together

Echolocation—using sound to sense objects

Roost—a place where bats rest during the daytime

You might encourage students to do some research on their own nonfiction topics, looking in glossaries and in the bodies of texts they are using to research to see if they can find some domain-specific words that they could use in their pieces.

6. Text Structures

Writing Bird by Bird

In one of my favorite mentor texts, *Bird by Bird: Some Instructions on Writing and Life*, Anne Lamott (1994) writes about her older brother as a child, sitting at the kitchen table, close to tears, trying to write a report on birds that was due the next day (but assigned three months prior). His father sat down next to him, put his arm around his shoulder, and said, "'Bird by bird, buddy. Just take it bird by bird'" (19).

Sometimes we get overwhelmed and don't know where to start, like Anne Lamott's brother. Once we find our focus, breaking down the large parts into smaller chunks and organizational structures—chapters, sections, vignettes—can be a great way to create footholds, or little steps, that can ease us into writing, bird by bird.

TYPES OF NONFICTION TEXT STRUCTURES

Nonfiction writers use many kinds of structures and ways of organizing ideas, and often a nonfiction piece is a combination of several. Here are a few, described in more detail later:

* description of features, characteristics, or examples
* chronological sequence

* problem and solution

* compare and contrast

* cause and effect

Description of features, characteristics, or examples Some writers describe a topic, idea, person, place, or thing by listing its features, characteristics, or examples.

James Cross Giblin (2004) describes the sphinx in *Secrets of the Sphinx* with precise details (see the excerpt in the next section, "Chronological Sequence"), but his description does something else: it follows a sequence of the sun rising on and illuminating it.

Nonfiction writers use many kinds of structures and ways of organizing ideas, and often a nonfiction piece is a combination of several.

Chronological sequence When using chronological sequence, a writer describes items or events in order, or tells the steps to follow to do something or make something.

Look at the sequence of the sun rising on the sphinx in this excerpt. What items, events, or steps are listed? Notice also how descriptive Giblin's details are:

> *First*, the huge paws of a lion appear, *followed* by the animal's powerful haunches and shoulders. *As the sun rises higher*, the creature's face catches the light. But it is not the face of a lion. No, it is the face of a man. A man with broad lips, a broken nose, and eyes that gaze steadily forward. A man wearing the flared headdress of an ancient Egyptian pharaoh. (2004, 4; emphasis added)

Problem and solution Sometimes a nonfiction writer tells about a problem (and sometimes says why there is a problem) and then gives one or more possible solutions. A piece organized in this way might answer the following questions:

* What is the problem?

* Why is this a problem?

* Is anything being done to solve the problem?

* What can be done to solve the problem?

Marching for Freedom: Walk Together, Children, and Don't You Grow Weary (Partridge 2009) is an example of the problem-and-solution structure in narrative form.

The problem, as Elizabeth Partridge states in the first chapter, "Voteless, 1963," is that African Americans weren't allowed to vote in 1963 because of racist laws. The solution to the problem is detailed in the subsequent chapters, which describe how Martin Luther King Jr., and many other courageous people, fought for the right to vote. The fight ended with the passage of the Voting Rights Act of 1965, the topic of the last chapter in the book.

Compare and contrast When comparing and contrasting, a nonfiction writer shows how two different things are alike and how they are different. A nonfiction piece organized this way will answer the following questions:

  * What things are being compared?

  * In what ways are they alike?

  * In what ways are they different?

Seymour Simon's *Whales* compares and contrasts whales with other aquatic animals and with humans:

> *Whales are not fish*, as some people mistakenly think. Fish are cold-blooded animals. This means their body temperature changes with their surroundings. *Whales are mammals* that live in the sea. *Like cats, dogs, monkeys, and people, whales are warm-blooded.*
>
> *A fish breathes by taking in water* and passing it through gills to extract oxygen, *but a whale must surface to inhale air* into its lungs. (1999, 6; emphasis added)

Cause and effect Cause is *why* something happened. Effect is *what* happened. A nonfiction writer using this structure will answer the following questions:

  * What happened?

  * Why did it happen?

  * What caused it to happen?

The Case of the Vanishing Golden Frogs: A Scientific Mystery, by Sandra Markle (2011) is about why the national symbol of Panama, the golden frog, started to disappear. The book describes Sandra Markle's search to figure out what caused the frogs to die.

CHAPTERS AND SECTIONS: BREAKING WRITING INTO PARTS

Dividing a topic into chapters and making a table of contents is another way for nonfiction writers to structure and organize. Subdividing the chapters in the table of contents into smaller units with subheadings can help nonfiction writers tackle a complex topic.

Sophie Webb chronicles her four-month-long journey to the Eastern Tropical Pacific Ocean to study seabirds and marine mammals in *Far from Shore: Chronicles of an Open Ocean Voyage* (2011). Webb organizes the chapters cleverly into month, location, and latitude and longitude, so the chapters read like a sailor's logbook:

July—San Diego, California

32"73' North Latitude, 117"17' West Longitude

A Day Offshore

13"13' N, 122
47' W

Kathryn Lasky divides *The Man Who Made Time Travel* (2003) into short three- to four-paragraph vignettes that help the reader digest a lot of discipline-specific content as well as new vocabulary. Here are some of her distinct and engaging chapter titles: "A Stormy Night"; "A Matter of Time"; "The Prize"; "Tiptoes and Bleeding Dogs."

WRITING TIP

Webbing to Break Large Pieces of Information into Smaller Parts

I frequently use webbing to help break down large amounts of information into categories. Ask each student to place his or her topic in the middle of a page in a circle with lines drawn from the center. If students have been engaged in research, they can begin to think about the larger chunks of information they could integrate to create chapters emanating from the circle in the middle.

Elizabeth Partridge arranges the historical narrative in *Marching for Freedom* (2009) chronologically by day and date, culminating in the last chapter, which is the date of the passing of the Voting Rights Act on August 6, 1965:

Contents

Voteless, 1963

Martin Luther King Jr. Arrives, 1965

      January 2

      January 4–14

      January 18–22

      February 1–17

      February 19–March 6

Bloody Sunday: March 7, 1965

Turn Around Tuesday: March 9

Day One: Sunday, March 21

Day Two: Monday, March 22

Day Three: Tuesday, March 23

Day Four: Wednesday, March 24

Day Five: Thursday, March 25

Voting Rights Act: August 6, 1965

LINKS TO THE COMMON CORE STATE STANDARDS: STRUCTURE AND ORGANIZATION

English Language Arts Standards: Writing

All emphasis added.

Text Types and Purposes

3–5

CCSS.ELA-Literacy.W.3.1: Write **opinion pieces** on topics or texts, supporting a point of view with reasons.

CCSS.ELA-Literacy.W.4.1, 5.1: Write **opinion pieces** on topics or texts, supporting a point of view with reasons and information.

> **CCSS.ELA-Literacy.W.3.1a:** Introduce the topic or text they are writing about, state an opinion, and *create an organizational structure that lists reasons*.

> **CCSS.ELA-Literacy.W.4.1a:** Introduce a topic or text clearly, state an opinion, and *create an organizational structure in which related ideas are grouped to support the writer's purpose*.

> **CCSS.ELA-Literacy.W.5.1a:** Introduce a topic or text clearly, state an opinion, and *create an organizational structure in which ideas are logically grouped to support the writer's purpose*.

CCSS.ELA-Literacy.W.3.2, 4.2, 5.2: Write **informative/explanatory texts** to examine a topic and convey ideas and information clearly.

> **CCSS.ELA-Literacy.W.3.2a:** Introduce a topic and *group related information together*; include illustrations when useful to aiding comprehension.

> **CCSS.ELA-Literacy.W.4.2a, 5.2a:** Introduce a topic clearly and *group related information in paragraphs and sections*; include formatting (e.g., headings), illustrations, and multimedia when useful to aiding comprehension.

CCSS.ELA-Literacy.W.3.3, 4.3, 5.3: Write **narratives** to develop real or imagined experiences or events using effective technique, descriptive details, and clear event sequences.

> **CCSS.ELA-Literacy.W.3.3a:** Establish a situation and introduce a narrator and/or characters; *organize an event sequence that unfolds naturally*.

> **CCSS.ELA-Literacy.W.4.3a, 5.3a:** Orient the reader by establishing a situation and introducing a narrator and/or characters; *organize an event sequence that unfolds naturally*.

6–8

CCSS.ELA-Literacy.W.6.2: Write **informative/explanatory texts** to examine a topic and convey ideas, concepts, and information through the selection, organization, and analysis of relevant content.

> **CCSS.ELA-Literacy.W.6.2a:** Introduce a topic; *organize ideas*, concepts, and information, using strategies such as definition, classification, *comparison/contrast*, and *cause/effect*; include formatting (e.g., headings), graphics (e.g., charts, tables), and multimedia when useful to aiding comprehension.
>
> **CCSS.ELA-Literacy.W.7.2a, 8.2a:** Introduce a topic clearly, previewing what is to follow; *organize ideas*, concepts, and information, using strategies such as definition, classification, *comparison/contrast*, and *cause/effect*; include formatting (e.g., headings), graphics (e.g., charts, tables), and multimedia when useful to aiding comprehension.

CCSS.ELA-Literacy.W.6.3, 7.3, 8.3: Write **narratives** to develop real or imagined experiences or events using effective technique, relevant descriptive details, and well-structured event sequences.

> **CCSS.ELA-Literacy.W.6.3a:** Engage and orient the reader by establishing a context and introducing a narrator and/or characters; organize an event sequence that unfolds naturally and logically.
>
> **CCSS.ELA-Literacy.W.7.3a, 8.3a:** Engage and orient the reader by establishing a context and point of view and introducing a narrator and/or characters; organize an event sequence that unfolds naturally and logically.

Try This Structuring and Organizing Nonfiction

Gather a bunch of nonfiction mentor texts and ask students to determine the structure and organization of each text by reading the table of contents, if there is one, and flipping through the pages to see if there are chapters, subheadings, vignettes, paragraphs, or other ways of organizing the text. Ask students to try to determine the book's structure and organization without reading the entire book. Just reading a book's table of contents can give the reader an idea of how the author organized the material.

As students prepare to write their own nonfiction pieces, they can brainstorm ways they would like to organize their writing, perhaps inspired by mentor texts.

7. Endings

Letting Words Linger

How important are endings in the movies we watch? Two people get together and ride into the sunset; a criminal is caught and put behind bars; an illness is cured; some huge problem is finally resolved. Readers, just like movie watchers, like an ending that feels resolved or gives them something to ponder. Many writers, including myself, spend a lot of time on the leads of our nonfiction pieces. But just as important is how we conclude our pieces, and what we leave the reader with.

Students can begin to ask themselves about their endings when they first begin writing their nonfiction pieces. They can ask:

* Do I know what my ending will be like?

* What do I want to leave the reader with?

* Where do I want this nonfiction piece to end up?

* How can I inspire my reader at the end?

William Zinsser says about endings, "The positive reason for ending well is that a good last sentence—or last paragraph, is a joy in itself. It gives the reader a lift, and it lingers when the article is over" (2006, 64).

TYPES OF ENDINGS

Circular ending A circular ending is one that echoes back to the lead some-how. Usually, the repetition back to the lead means that the book has taught the reader something in between, so by the end things have changed. In *Surprising Sharks*, Nicola Davies (2003) changes the idea that sharks are dangerous to humans to the idea that humans are dangerous to sharks:

Readers, just like movie watchers, like an ending that feels resolved or gives them something to ponder.

Lead

You're swimming in the warm blue sea. What's the one word that turns your dream into a nightmare? What's the one word that makes you think of a giant man-eating killer? Shaaaaarrrkk! (6)

Ending

If you were a shark swimming in the lovely blue sea, the last word you'd want to hear would be . . . human! (27)

Question ending A lead that ends with a question often asks the reader to ponder even after she has finished the book. Sometimes the question is meant to compel the reader to act, like in Seymour Simon's *Whales*:

Will whales be allowed to remain to share the world with us? The choice is ours. (1999, 40)

Chronological ending If you're writing a nonfiction narrative, the ending can be the chronological finish of the event or subject. A personal narrative usually ends when the story ends but often has some kind of emotional revelation or summation by the author.

WRITING TIP

Studying a Variety of Endings

Students can read endings from several nonfiction mentor texts, including the examples in the reproducible on page 107, and discuss how other authors create strong endings.

Quotation ending Another way to end a nonfiction piece is by using a quotation that is usually an inspiring or surprising quote from someone referenced in the text or a quote that summarizes the ideas that you've presented to the reader. Richard Michelson's book *As Good as Anybody* (2008) ends with an inspiring quote by Abraham Joshua Heschel to Martin Luther King Jr. when they marched together in Selma, Alabama, in 1965 against racism and anti-Semitism:

> Martin took a step forward. Abraham took a step beside him. "This too is God's work," Abraham told Martin. "I feel like my legs are praying."

Thoughtful and reflective ending My least favorite ending is the *summation*—when the author states, "In summary . . . ," or "To conclude. . . ." I know many students are taught to end essays this way, but that kind of ending is too formulaic and bores the reader. Instead, a writer can add one final bit of information or idea—or provide a thoughtful and reflective conclusion that the reader can ponder, as Jeanette Winter does in *The Watcher: Jane Goodall's Life with the Chimps* (2011):

> She talked to the animals like Dr. Doolittle,
> and walked unafraid like Tarzan,
> and watched and wrote,
> and opened a window for us
> to the world of the chimpanzees.

LINKS TO THE COMMON CORE STATE STANDARDS: ENDINGS

English Language Arts Standards: Writing

All emphasis added.

3–5

CCSS.ELA-Literacy.W.3.1: Write **opinion pieces** on topics or texts, supporting a point of view with reasons.

> **CCSS.ELA-Literacy.W.3.1d:** Provide a *concluding statement or section.*

CCSS.ELA-Literacy.W.4.1, 5.1: Write **opinion pieces** on topics or texts, supporting a point of view with reasons and information.

> **CCSS.ELA-Literacy.W.4.1d, 5.1d:** Provide a *concluding statement or section* related to the opinion presented.

CCSS.ELA-Literacy.W.3.2, 4.2, 5.2: Write **informative/explanatory texts** to examine a topic and convey ideas and information clearly.

> **CCSS.ELA-Literacy.W.3.2d:** Provide a *concluding statement or section.*

> **CCSS.ELA-Literacy.W.4.2e, 5.2e:** Provide a *concluding statement or section* related to the information or explanation presented.

CCSS.ELA-Literacy.W.3.3, 4.3, 5.3: Write **narratives** to develop real or imagined experiences or events using effective technique, descriptive details, and clear event sequences.

> **CCSS.ELA-Literacy.W.3.3d:** Provide a *sense of closure.*

> **CCSS.ELA-Literacy.W.4.3e, 5.3e:** Provide a *conclusion that follows from the narrated experiences or events.*

6–8

CCSS.ELA-Literacy.W.7.2, 8.2: Write **informative/explanatory texts** to examine a topic and convey ideas, concepts, and information through the selection, organization, and analysis of relevant content.

> **CCSS.ELA-Literacy.W.6.2f, 7.2f, 8.2f:** Provide a *concluding statement or section* that follows from the information or explanation presented.

CCSS.ELA-Literacy.W.6.3, 7.3, 8.3: Write **narratives** to develop real or imagined experiences or events using effective technique, relevant descriptive details, and well-structured event sequences.

> **CCSS.ELA-Literacy.W.6.3e, 7.3e, 8.3e:** Provide a *conclusion that follows from the narrated experiences or events.*

Literacy in History/Social Studies, Science, and Technical Subjects

CCSS.ELA-Literacy.WHST.6–8.2: Write **informative/explanatory texts**, including the narration of historical events, scientific procedures/experiments, or technical processes.

> **CCSS.ELA-Literacy.WHST. 6–8.2f:** Provide a *concluding statement or section* that follows from and supports the information or explanation presented.

Endings

Circular Ending

Lead

You're swimming in the warm blue sea. What's the one word that turns your dream into a nightmare? What's the one word that makes you think of a giant man-eating killer? Shaaaaarrrkk! (Nicola Davies, *Surprising Sharks*, 2003, 6)

Ending

If you were a shark swimming in the lovely blue sea, the last word you'd want to hear would be . . . human! (Nicola Davies, *Surprising Sharks*, 2003, 27)

Question Ending

Will whales be allowed to remain to share the world with us? The choice is ours. (Seymour Simon, *Whales*, 1999, 40)

Quotation Ending

Martin took a step forward. Abraham took a step beside him. "This too is God's work," Abraham told Martin. "I feel like my legs are praying." (Richard Michelson, *As Good as Anybody: Martin Luther King Jr. and Abraham Joshua Heschel's Amazing March Toward Freedom*, 2008)

Thoughtful and Reflective Ending

She talked to the animals like Dr. Doolittle,
and walked unafraid like Tarzan,
and watched and wrote,
and opened a window for us
to the world of the chimpanzees.
(Jeanette Winter, *The Watcher: Jane Goodall's Life with the Chimps*, 2011)

Nuts and Bolts

More Tools of the Nonfiction Trade

I've gathered some additional nonfiction tools in this section, including nonfiction text features, dialogue and quotes from primary source material, truth and accuracy in nonfiction, sentences of varying length, linking words, and source citations and bibliographies. These tools don't necessarily fall into one of the seven essential craft tool categories but are nevertheless valuable for nonfiction writers.

You might dip into the "Nuts and Bolts" section to find ideas to present as mini-lessons to the whole group or small groups or to use in one-on-one conferences to stretch or challenge more experienced writers.

USING NONFICTION TEXT FEATURES IN MEANINGFUL WAYS

Nonfiction text features are tools, unique to nonfiction, that help organize information, support readability, or direct a reader's attention. They are found mostly in informative, or explanatory, texts and in nonfiction picture books, and sometimes in other nonfiction texts such as biographies and historical texts. In many classrooms, teachers introduce text features first, or instead of, writing craft tools such as leads and precise language. I wanted to de-emphasize text features because although bright fonts and dramatic visuals make nonfiction enticing to a reader and can aid in comprehension, they should first and foremost support a well-written nonfiction text.

I focus on four that are most common:

1. Headings
2. Table of contents
3. Captions for visuals
4. Graphics: diagrams, charts, tables, and maps

Headings Headings can be chapter titles or simple labels that tell the reader what the focus of a section of writing is. A heading is usually found at the top of a page and is usually in bold or in a different color. Creating headings starts with organizing work that will help focus large pieces of information into smaller pieces (see "Chapters and Sections: Breaking Writing into Parts," on page 98). Once writing is organized into smaller units, students should try being imaginative, clear, and descriptive when writing their headings; for example, here are a few headings from *Bugs: A Close-Up Look at Insects and Their Relatives* (Malyan 2005):

Fast Flier

Watch Me Run

Babysitting Bugs

Flutter, Flutter

To help students practice writing headings, cover a heading in a nonfiction book with a piece of paper and read a short passage beneath the heading, then ask students to brainstorm possible headings for that passage. Afterward, they can discuss which option works best, and compare their ideas with the heading in the book. They can then brainstorm possible headings for their own writing.

Table of contents A table of contents is helpful when you have gathered similar information into chapters or under headings. A table of contents is always located within the first few pages of a text and gives the reader the page numbers of the chapters or sections. Even before a student begins to write, he can create a table of contents to help organize information; then he can revise it as he continues to write.

Captions   Captions appear beneath, above, or next to graphic images and give information about what is being visually presented. A caption can be a simple label or fact, an elaborate description, or a creative and informative part of the text. In *Bugs: A Close-Up Look at Insects and Their Relatives* (Malyan 2005), the captions, accompanying the remarkable photographs of insects and bugs, are written in the first-person point of view from the perspective of the insects or bugs. The caption next to a vivid close-up of a caterpillar reads, "I've got 12 eyes, but I can only see if it's light or dark" (7). Encourage students to be creative and descriptive, yet factually accurate, when writing their captions.

Show students a photograph from a nonfiction book, cover up the caption with a piece of paper, and ask them to brainstorm and write a descriptive yet informative caption to accompany the photograph. They can then compare their ideas with the caption in the book.

Graphics such as diagrams, charts, tables, and maps are the visual "show, don't tell" tools of nonfiction writing and are used when words can't provide the information or if the information needs more detail.

Graphics   Graphics such as diagrams, charts, tables, and maps are the visual "show, don't tell" tools of nonfiction writing and are used when words can't provide the information or if the information needs more detail. Graphics are meant to be read and add informational content to a nonfiction text; that is, they are not optional reading. If, for example, I want to show the different parts of a shark, I can include a labeled diagram instead of using words to describe the parts of a shark. Or if I want to show where bullfrogs live in the United States, I can show a map with illustrations or photographs of bullfrogs placed on the geographic areas where they live.

Young nonfiction writers tend to want to fill their nonfiction texts with diagrams and other graphics. One or two well-placed diagrams accompanied by labels usually provide the information that the reader needs.

After writing a draft of a nonfiction text, a student can reread and make decisions as to where and what type of well-placed graphics could add more detail to the text.

LINKS TO THE COMMON CORE STATE STANDARDS: TEXT FEATURES

English Language Arts Standards: Writing

All emphasis added.

Text Types and Purposes: Informative/Explanatory Texts

3–5

CCSS.ELA-Literacy.W.3.2a: Introduce a topic and group related information together; include *illustrations* when useful to aiding comprehension.

CCSS.ELA-Literacy.W.4.2a: Introduce a topic clearly and group related information in paragraphs and sections; include *formatting (e.g., headings), illustrations,* and multimedia when useful to aiding comprehension.

CCSS.ELA-Literacy.W.5.2a: Introduce a topic clearly, provide a general observation and focus, and group related information logically; include *formatting (e.g., headings), illustrations,* and multimedia when useful to aiding comprehension.

6–8

CCSS.ELA-Literacy.W.6.2a: Introduce a topic; organize ideas, concepts, and information, using strategies such as definition, classification, comparison/contrast, and cause/effect; include *formatting (e.g., headings), graphics (e.g., charts, tables),* and multimedia when useful to aiding comprehension.

CCSS.ELA-Literacy.W.7.2a: Introduce a topic clearly, previewing what is to follow; organize ideas, concepts, and information, using strategies such as definition, classification, comparison/contrast, and cause/effect; include *formatting (e.g., headings), graphics (e.g., charts, tables),* and multimedia when useful to aiding comprehension.

CCSS.ELA-Literacy.W.8.2a: Introduce a topic clearly, previewing what is to follow; organize ideas, concepts, and information into broader categories; include *formatting (e.g., headings), graphics (e.g., charts, tables),* and multimedia when useful to aiding comprehension.

Literacy in History/Social Studies, Science, and Technical Subjects

CCSS.ELA-Literacy.WHST.6–8.2a: Introduce a topic clearly, previewing what is to follow; organize ideas, concepts, and information into broader categories as appropriate to achieving purpose; include *formatting (e.g., headings), graphics (e.g., charts, tables),* and multimedia when useful to aiding comprehension.

USING DIALOGUE AND QUOTES FROM PRIMARY SOURCE MATERIAL

Many nonfiction writers sprinkle their writing with quotes from either experts in the field, eyewitnesses, or primary sources such as letters, journals, and documents. Nonfiction writers do this for many reasons; quotes can strengthen writing by adding validity to facts and information, and they can add humanity and warmth. Quotes from eyewitnesses can make information more believable and can capture a subject's personality. It's through what a person says, including dialect, clichés, and other nuances, that his or her personality comes alive.

Titanic: Voices from the Disaster, by Deborah Hopkinson (2012), is based on firsthand recollections of survivors and other primary sources such as the wreckage report from the *Titanic*, which thread throughout the narrative and put a human face on the tragedy.

Beginning a chapter with a quote that relates to the content of the text is also an effective way to make a nonfiction text more authentic, offer a preview of what the chapter will be about, or add an extra spark of inspiration to a text. For example:

Chapter 1: Declarations of Independence

"Liberty, when it begins to take root, is a plant of rapid growth."—George Washington (Nelson 2011, 9)

A quote from a primary source such as a journal, a letter, or a document can support and strengthen a narrative or facts, as does the quote from Columbus' journal in this excerpt:

Finally, the men demanded that Columbus turn back and head for home. When he refused, some of the sailors whispered together of mutiny. They wanted to kill the admiral by throwing him overboard. But, for the moment, the crisis passed. Columbus managed to calm his men and persuade them to be patient a while longer.

"I am having serious trouble with the crew . . . complaining that they will never be able to return home," he wrote in his journal. "They have said that it is insanity and suicidal on their part to risk their lives following the

WRITING TIP

Formatting Quotations

If you're interviewing an expert, or quoting from a speech or letter, it's important to use a person's exact words. You don't have to include the whole quote, especially if it's lengthy—only the part that gets your point across or captures the person's personality. You can include a partial quote using ellipses for the parts of the quote you leave out. Writers sometimes paraphrase a quote if it's too long.

The length of a quotation determines its formatting. If the quote is longer than one or two sentences, then it needs to be formatted in a block—set apart, single spaced, indented from both sides, separated from the sentences before and after by a space. If a quote is only one or two sentences, it should be incorporated into the paragraph and separated by a comma and quotation marks.

madness of a foreigner. . . . I am told by a few trusted men (and these are few in number!) that if I persist in going onward, the best course of action will be to throw me into the sea some night." (Freedman 2007, 2)

Some picture book writers fictionalize quotes, re-creating what might have been said, such as in *Amelia and Eleanor Go for a Ride*, by Pam Muñoz Ryan (1999). The book was inspired by a true event—an impromptu nighttime airplane ride that Amelia Earhart gave to Eleanor Roosevelt when Amelia was invited to the White House for dinner—and is based on diaries, book transcripts, and newspaper accounts. It also includes some fictional touches, like this dialogue: "So when Eleanor discovered that her friend Amelia was coming to town to give a speech, she naturally said, 'Bring your husband and come to dinner at my house! You can even sleep over'" (1). It may not be an exact quote of Eleanor Roosevelt's, but it conveys information that could be true, based on historical events.

The most effective way to use quotes in nonfiction is to thread the quotes throughout a well-written text. One of my favorite examples of weaving quotes seamlessly throughout a narrative is Candace Fleming's *Amelia Lost: The Life and Disappearance of Amelia Earhart* (2011). Fleming enhances her dramatic narrative with quotes from Amelia Earhart's last recorded radio transmission and recollections of a crew member on the coast guard cutter *Itasca* who was waiting for Earhart's plane. The effect is a harrowing and heartbreaking account of the moment Amelia Earhart was lost forever:

> Then—forty-five anxious minutes later—she was back:
> 8:45 A.M.: "WE ARE ON LINE 157–337. WE WILL REPEAT MESSAGE. . . . WE ARE RUNNING ON LINE NORTH AND SOUTH."
>
> The fear in Earhart's voice made Leo Bellarts's skin prickle. "I'm telling you, it sounded as if she would have broken out in a scream. . . . She was about ready to break into tears and go into hysterics. . . . I'll never forget it."
>
> Seconds turned to minutes. Minutes became an hour. But the sky above Howland Island remained empty.
>
> And in the radio room, Leo Bellarts and the other crew members sat listening to the "mournful sound of that static."
>
> Where, they wondered, was Amelia Earhart? (5)

The most effective way to use quotes in nonfiction is to thread the quotes throughout a well-written text.

LINKS TO THE COMMON CORE STATE STANDARDS: QUOTATIONS
English Language Arts Standards: Writing

All emphasis added.

Text Types and Purposes

CCSS.ELA-Literacy.W.4.2: Write **informative/explanatory texts** to examine a topic and convey ideas and information clearly.

> **CCSS.ELA-Literacy.W.4.2b, 5.2b:** Develop the topic with facts, definitions, concrete details, *quotations*, or other information and examples related to the topic.

CCSS.ELA-Literacy.W.6.2: Write **informative/explanatory texts** to examine a topic and convey ideas, concepts, and information through the selection, organization, and analysis of relevant content.

> **CCSS.ELA-Literacy.W.6.2b, 7.2b, 8.2b:** Develop the topic with relevant facts, definitions, concrete details, *quotations*, or other information and examples.

Literacy in History/Social Studies, Science, and Technical Subjects: Writing

CCSS.ELA-Literacy.WHST.6–8.2: Write **informative/explanatory texts**, including the narration of historical events, scientific procedures/ experiments, or technical processes.

> **CCSS.ELA-Literacy. WHST.6–8.2b:** Develop the topic with relevant, well-chosen facts, definitions, concrete details, *quotations*, or other information and examples.

English Language Arts Standards: Language

CCSS.ELA-Literacy.L.3.2, 4.2: Demonstrate command of the conventions of standard English capitalization, punctuation, and spelling when writing.

> **CCSS.ELA-Literacy.L.3.2c:** Use commas and *quotation marks in dialogue.*

> **CCSS.ELA-Literacy.L.4.2b:** Use commas and *quotation marks to mark direct speech and quotations from a text.*

Ensuring Truth and Accuracy

On the blog *I.N.K.* (*Interesting Nonfiction for Kids*), Rosalyn Schanzer writes, "In nonfiction, you can never *ever* embellish the truth or make anything up, so every single detail in every single book has to be accurate" (2013).

Ultimately, it comes down to the issue of trust. We must be able to trust that a nonfiction writer is telling the facts accurately and truthfully.

But sometimes, particularly in narrative nonfiction, the issue of truth and accuracy gets tricky if the writer is fictionalizing scenes to get a larger point across. For example, in Lynne Cherry's *The Great Kapok Tree: A Tale of the Amazon Rain Forest* (2000), Cherry gives the boa constrictor a voice to make a broader point of what happens to the rain forest and its creatures when rain forests are destroyed, and to help readers relate to this issue on a more intimate level:

> A boa constrictor lived in the kapok tree. He slithered down its trunk to where the man was sleeping. He looked at the gash the ax had made in the trees. Then the huge snake slid very close to the man and hissed in his ear: "Senhor, this tree is a tree of miracles. It is my home, where generations of my ancestors have lived. Do not chop it down."

Sounds and rhythm are invisible tools in nonfiction writing, but just as important as figurative language and imagery in making writing come to life.

As a writing community, you need to discuss and make a decision about whether or not adding fictionalized touches to nonfiction is acceptable. If, for example, students are immersed in a historical fiction writing unit, the discussion might center on how the characters may be fictionalized for the purposes of narrative. Or the class could decide if adding dialogue to an informational text on animals is acceptable, as in *The Great Kapok Tree*. A discussion of the similarities and differences between fiction and nonfiction might be a good place to begin your nonfiction unit of study, and a way to establish the writing parameters for nonfiction truth and accuracy.

Varying Sentence Length

Sounds and rhythm are invisible tools in nonfiction writing, but just as important as figurative language and imagery in making writing come to life. Like the hum of a refrigerator (but more varied and musical), the sound of our words and sentences is invisible and yet very present. Nonfiction writers develop an awareness of the rhythm and sounds of words and sentences, and we listen to the pace of our sentences. Usually, we use short sentences and paragraphs for fast-paced action and longer sentences and paragraphs for a slower unfolding of events.

Roy Peter Clark (2013b) says, "The problem of course, is boredom. Readers like things that move, move, move. This requires a variety of sentences, written at different lengths."

As a journalist, he also advises that writers vary their sentence length for dramatic effect. He offers an example of a scene from war, by journalist Richard Ben Cramer: "When the bombs hit, even though they are two-thirds of a mile away, the air in the shelter vibrates with a sound too low to hear. The glasses rattle. The talk stops" (Clark 2013a).

Here's another example, from an informational picture book. Listen to the pace of the first three pages of *Bat Loves the Night*, by Nicola Davies (2001a). This fairly long opening sentence's rhythm is proselike and reads as a long, flowing sentence:

> Bat is waking,
> upside down as usual,
> hanging by her toenails.

Davies follows the first long sentence with three short ones and succeeds in varying the length and pace of the rhythm.

> Her beady eyes open.
> Her pixie ears twitch.
> She shakes her thistledown fur.

Once again, Davies varies the pace and length of her sentences, which gives her words musical variety. And then she drops in the short sentence to give it emphasis.

> Now she unhooks her toes
> and drops into black space.
> With a sound like a tiny umbrella
> opening, she flaps her wings.

> Bat is flying.

As students read their favorite nonfiction authors, ask them to become aware of sentence length. Ask them to mark short and long sentences they find the most effective.

As students write, they can vary the rhythm of their own sentences. They can write a passage in short, staccato sentences and then write the same paragraph using long, melodious words and flowing sentences.

LINKS TO THE COMMON CORE STATE STANDARDS: TRANSITION WORDS AND PHRASES

One of the most challenging jobs of a nonfiction writer is to learn to connect statements and sentences together in ways that make prose easier for the reader to follow. Writing that doesn't employ transition, or linking, words is often short and choppy. Linking words help prose flow, help writers elaborate on a point or fact, but can also signal to the reader that the writing is about to take another turn or line of thought.

The Common Core State Standards for writing include the use of linking or transition words. For example, in grade 3, most of the linking words for informative/explanatory writing show how one idea builds on another, helping the writer elaborate a point or idea she is making: *also, another, and, more.* The word *but* is a linking word that signals a contrast, such as when students are writing compare-and-contrast pieces.

The linking words cited in the CCSS for writing informative/explanatory texts in grade 4 also show how one idea builds on another, except for the word *because*, which shows a consequence or result.

Grade 5 standards for writing informative/explanatory texts introduce two more linking phrases: *in contrast* and *especially. In contrast* shows the reader a contrasting idea or point of view, and *especially* is used to show emphasis.

In grade 6, the CCSS for writing informative/explanatory texts states that writers, "Use appropriate transitions to clarify the relationships among ideas and concepts." Each standard emphasizes different transition words depending on the text type. For example, again in grade 6, the standard for writing narratives emphasizes transition words that show time, like the examples given under the head "Words That Show Time Shifts and Sequencing" in the Writing Tip on page 120.

English Language Arts Standards: Writing

The following standards refer to linking words.

All emphasis added.

3–5

CCSS.ELA-Literacy.W.3.1: Write **opinion pieces** on topics or texts, supporting a point of view with reasons.

> **CCSS.ELA-Literacy.W.3.1c:** *Use linking words and phrases* (e.g., *because, therefore, since, for example*) to connect opinion and reasons.

CCSS.ELA-Literacy.W.4.1, 5.1: Write **opinion pieces** on topics or texts, supporting a point of view with reasons and information.

> **CCSS.ELA-Literacy.W.4.1c:** *Link* opinion and reasons *using words and phrases* (e.g., *for instance, in order to, in addition*).

> **CCSS.ELA-Literacy.W.5.1c:** *Link* opinion and reasons *using words, phrases, and clauses* (e.g., *consequently, specifically*).

CCSS.ELA-Literacy.W.3.2, 4.2, 5.2: Write **informative/explanatory texts** to examine a topic and convey ideas and information clearly.

> **CCSS.ELA-Literacy.W.3.2c:** Use *linking words and phrases* (e.g., *also, another, and, more, but*) to connect ideas within categories of information.

> **CCSS.ELA-Literacy.W.4.2c:** *Link ideas* within categories of information *using words and phrases* (e.g., *another, for example, also, because*).

> **CCSS.ELA-Literacy.W.5.2c:** *Link ideas* within and across categories of information *using words, phrases, and clauses* (e.g., *in contrast, especially*).

CCSS.ELA-Literacy.W.3.3: Write narratives to develop real or imagined experiences or events using effective technique, descriptive details, and clear event sequences.

> **CCSS.ELA-Literacy.W.3.3c:** Use *temporal words and phrases* to signal event order.

> **CCSS.ELA-Literacy.W.4.3c:** Use a variety of *transitional words and phrases* to manage the sequence of events.

> **CCSS.ELA-Literacy.W.5.3c:** Use a variety of *transitional words, phrases, and clauses* to manage the sequence of events.

6–8

CCSS.ELA-Literacy.W.6.2: Write **informative/explanatory texts** to examine a topic and convey ideas, concepts, and information through the selection, organization, and analysis of relevant content.

> **CCSS.ELA-Literacy.W.6.2c:** *Use appropriate transitions* to clarify the relationships among ideas and concepts.

> **CCSS.ELA-Literacy.W.7.2c:** *Use appropriate transitions* to create cohesion and clarify the relationships among ideas and concepts.

> **CCSS.ELA-Literacy.W.8.2c:** *Use appropriate and varied transitions* to create cohesion and clarify the relationships among ideas and concepts.

CCSS.ELA-Literacy.W.6.3: Write **narratives** to develop real or imagined experiences or events using effective technique, relevant descriptive details, and well-structured event sequences.

> **CCSS.ELA-Literacy.W.6.3c:** *Use a variety of transition words, phrases, and clauses* to convey sequence and signal shifts from one time frame or setting to another.

> **CCSS.ELA-Literacy.W.7.3c:** *Use appropriate transitions to create cohesion and clarify* the relationships among ideas and concepts.

> **CCSS.ELA-Literacy.W.8.3c:** *Use a variety of transition words, phrases, and clauses* to convey sequence, signal shifts from one time frame or setting to another, and show the relationships among experiences and events.

WRITING TIP

Transition Words and Phrases

Words That Show Time Shifts and Sequencing

after	later
before	immediately
then	eventually
once	previously
at first	when
finally	soon after

Words That Show Summary

therefore	in short
finally	in conclusion
consequently	as a result

Words That Show Compare and Contrast

like	likewise
similar to	compared to
also	in contrast
unlike	contrasted with
similarly	however
in the same way	on the other hand

Words That Add Information

also	besides
another	furthermore
in addition	moreover
and	first, second, third

Citing Sources and Creating a Bibliography

It's important to give credit to the sources we use when we research nonfiction. We call this *citing sources*. It's only fair to give authors credit for coming up with ideas, or for their writing, and it gives our readers a list of where information came from. Starting in third grade, I ask students to begin the work of creating bibliographies. In third grade, students cite only the author and book or publication, but are not required to write a complete, formal bibliography with publisher and date. If students are keeping notebooks for notes and facts, I ask them to keep a page or two in the back to collect their sources as they are researching.

For students in older grades, I teach them the following format for creating a bibliography:

1. Author's last name, then author's first name, followed by a period. First letters of both names capitalized. (If there is more than one source cited, the list is arranged alphabetically by authors' last names.)

   Heard, Georgia.

2. Date, in parentheses, when the book was published, followed by a period.

   Heard, Georgia. **(2013).**

3. Exact title and subtitle of a book, underlined or italicized, with the first letter of each word capitalized (except for small and unimportant words like *a, to, an, and* as well as prepositions that are four letters or fewer: *at, of, but, by, in,* etc.), followed by a period. Poems, plays, and articles are not underlined but instead are put in quotation marks.

   Heard, Georgia. (2103). **<u>Finding the Heart of Nonfiction: Teaching 7 Essential Craft Tools with Mentor Texts.</u>**

4. Location of publishing company: city (capitalized) and then state abbreviation (capitalized), followed by a colon.

   Heard, Georgia. (2013). <u>Finding the Heart of Nonfiction: Teaching 7 Essential Craft Tools with Mentor Texts.</u> **Portsmouth, NH:**

5. Name of publishing company (capitalized), followed by a period.

   Heard, Georgia. (2013). <u>Finding the Heart of Nonfiction: Teaching 7 Essential Craft Tools with Mentor Texts.</u> Portsmouth, NH: **Heinemann.**

CONCLUSION

As I write, the books behind me—my mentor texts—fill my head and heart with exquisite language and make me see the world in new ways. Writers are first and foremost readers. We read to experience the world through someone else's heart, eyes, and mind. We read because it impels us to write our best. We read because that's how we learn to write.

My hope is that in reading *Finding the Heart of Nonfiction*, you and your students will be inspired by the words and craft lessons from the mentor texts I've chosen but also inspired to seek out your own mentor texts, to find your writing voices, and to continue to explore the world through nonfiction.

Works Cited and Bibliography

Mentor Texts Cited

Aronson, Marc. 2010. *If Stones Could Speak: Unlocking the Secrets of Stonehenge.* Washington, DC: National Geographic Children's Books.

———. 2012. *The Skull in the Rock: How a Scientist, a Boy, and Google Earth Opened a New Window on Human Origins.* Washington, DC: National Geographic Children's Books.

Aston, Dianna Hutts. 2007. *A Seed Is Sleepy.* San Francisco: Chronicle Books.

Bishop, Nic. 2008. *Frogs.* New York: Scholastic Nonfiction.

Black Ian Michael. 2010. *A Pig Parade Is a Terrible Idea.* New York: Simon & Schuster Books for Young Readers.

Boring, Mel. 1998. *Birds, Nests and Eggs.* Minnetonka, MN: NorthWord.

Brinckloe, Julie. 1986. *Fireflies!* New York: Aladdin.

Bryson, Bill. 2004. *A Short History of Nearly Everything.* New York: Broadway Books.

Butterworth, Chris. 2006. *Sea Horse: The Shyest Fish in the Sea.* Cambridge, MA: Candlewick.

Cherry, Lynne. 2000. *The Great Kapok Tree: A Tale of the Amazon Rain Forest.* Boston: Sandpiper/Houghton Mifflin Harcourt.

Columbia Electronic Encyclopedia. 2012. *Columbia Electronic Encyclopedia*, 6th edition, s.v. "frog."

Davies, Nicola. 2001a. *Bat Loves the Night.* Cambridge, MA: Candlewick.

———. 2001b. *One Tiny Turtle.* Cambridge, MA: Candlewick.

———. 2003. *Surprising Sharks.* Cambridge, MA: Candlewick.

Fleming, Candace. 2011. *Amelia Lost: The Life and Disappearance of Amelia Earhart.* New York: Schwartz and Wade Books.

Freedman, Russell. 1998. *Kids at Work: Lewis Hine and the Crusade Against Child Labor.* New York: Clarion Books.

———. 2007. *Who Was First? Discovering the Americas.* New York: Clarion Books.

George, Jean Craighead. 1996. *One Day in the Desert.* New York: HarperCollins.

———. 1997. *Everglades.* New York: HarperCollins.

Gibbons, Gail. 1990. *Beacons of Light: Lighthouses.* New York: Morrow Junior Books.

Giblin, James Cross. 2004. *Secrets of the Sphinx.* New York: Scholastic.

Gornick, Vivian. 2001. *The Situation and the Story: The Art of Personal Narrative.* New York: Farrar, Straus & Giroux.

Hart, Jack. 2007. *A Writer's Coach: The Complete Guide to Writing Strategies That Work*. New York: Anchor Books.

Heard, Georgia. 2013. "This Moment." In *Dare to Dream . . . Change the World*, ed. Jill Corcoran. San Diego: Kane Miller.

Heinz, Brian J. 2005. *Butternut Hollow Pond*. Minneapolis: First Avenue Editions.

Hirschmann, Kris. 2003. *Owls, Bats, Wolves and Other Nocturnal Animals*. New York: Scholastic.

Hopkinson, Deborah. 2012. *Titanic: Voices from the Disaster*. New York: Scholastic.

Kinney, Jeff. 2007. *Diary of a Wimpy Kid*. New York: Amulet Books.

Lamott, Anne. 1994. *Bird by Bird: Some Instructions on Writing and Life*. New York: Doubleday.

Lasky, Kathryn. 2003. *The Man Who Made Time Travel*. New York: Farrar, Straus, and Giroux.

Malyan, Sue. 2005. *Bugs: A Close-Up Look at Insects and Their Relatives*. New York: DK.

Markle, Sandra. 2011. *The Case of the Vanishing Golden Frogs: A Scientific Mystery*. Minneapolis: Milbrook.

McCullough, David. 2008. *John Adams*. New York: Simon and Schuster.

Michelson, Richard. 2008. *As Good as Anybody: Martin Luther King Jr. and Abraham Joshua Heschel's Amazing March Toward Freedom*. New York: Alfred A. Knopf.

Moss, Marissa. 2011. *Nurse, Soldier, Spy: The Story of Sarah Edmonds, a Civil War Hero*. New York: Abrams Books for Young Readers.

Nelson, Kadir. 2008. *We Are the Ship: The Story of Negro League Baseball*. New York: Hyperion Books.

———. 2011. *Heart and Soul: The Story of America and African Americans*. New York: Balzer and Bray.

Partridge, Elizabeth. 2009. *Marching for Freedom: Walk Together, Children, and Don't You Grow Weary*. New York: Viking Juvenile.

Paulsen, Gary. 2007. *Hatchet*. New York: Simon and Schuster Books for Young Readers.

Rappaport, Doreen. 2009. *Eleanor, Quiet No More: The Life of Eleanor Roosevelt*. New York: Hyperion Books for Children.

Ryan, Pam Muñoz. 1999. *Amelia and Eleanor Go for a Ride*. New York: Scholastic.

Simon, Seymour. 1999. *Whales*. Boston: Houghton Mifflin.

Stewart, Melissa. 2012. *Titanic*. Washington, DC: National Geographic Society.

Stone, Tanya Lee. 2009. *Almost Astronauts: Thirteen Women Who Dared to Dream.* Cambridge, MA: Candlewick.

Tavares, Matt. 2012. *Henry Aaron's Dream.* Cambridge, MA: Candlewick.

Telgemeier, Raina, and Ann M. Martin. 2006. *The Baby-Sitters Club: The Truth About Stacey.* New York: Graphix.

Thomas, Lewis. 1983. *Late Night Thoughts on Listening to Mahler's Ninth Symphony.* New York: Viking Press.

Tunnell, Michael O. 2010. *Candy Bomber: The Story of the Berlin Airlift's "Chocolate Pilot."* Watertown, MA: Charlesbridge.

Waring, Geoff. 2009. *Oscar and the Bat: A Book About Sound.* Cambridge, MA: Candlewick.

Webb, Sophie. 2011. *Far from Shore: Chronicles of an Open Ocean Voyage.* New York: Houghton Mifflin Books for Children.

Weitzman, David. 2010. *Skywalkers: Mohawk Ironworkers Build the City.* New York: Flash Point.

Whitehouse, David. 1999. "Walking on the Moon." *BBC News Online.* July 16. http://news.bbc.co.uk/2/hi/special_report/1999/07/99/the_moon_landing/394583.stm.

Winter, Jeanette. 2011. *The Watcher: Jane Goodall's Life with the Chimps.* New York: Schwartz and Wade Books.

Professional Works Cited

Clark, Roy Peter. 2013a. "Why the Late Richard Ben Cramer Was Such a Good Writer." How Tos. Poynter.org. www.poynter.org/how-tos/newsgathering-storytelling/writing-tools/199931/why-the-late-richard-ben-cramer-was-such-a-good-writer/.

———. 2013b. "How to Solve Your Most Difficult Writing Problems." Online chat. Poynter.org. February 21. www.poynter.org/how-tos/newsgathering-storytelling/writing-tools/204871/live-chat-today-get-help-solving-your-most-difficult-writing-problems/.

Didion, Joan. 1978. "The Art of Fiction No. 71." By Linda Kuehl. *The Paris Review* 74. www.theparisreview.org/interviews/3439/the-art-of-fiction-no-71-joan-didion.

Fredericks, Anthony D. 2003. "Evaluating and Using Nonfiction Literature in the Science Curriculum." In *Making Facts Come Alive: Choosing and Using Quality Nonfiction, K–8* (2d ed.), ed. Rosemary A. Bamford and Janice V. Kristo. Norwell, MA: Christopher-Gordon.

Hale, Constance. 2010. "What the Heck Is Narrative Journalism?" *Sin and Syntax* (blog). November 8. http://sinandsyntax.com/talking-story/narrative-journalism/.

Heard, Georgia. 1995. *Writing Toward Home: Tales and Lessons to Find Your Way.* Portsmouth, NH: Heinemann.

Heard, Georgia, and Jennifer McDonough. 2009. *A Place for Wonder: Reading and Writing Nonfiction in the Primary Grades.* Portland, ME: Stenhouse.

Lopate, Phillip. 2013. *To Show and to Tell: The Craft of Literary Nonfiction.* New York: Free Press.

Murray, Donald M. 2000. *Writing to Deadline: The Journalist at Work.* Portsmouth, NH: Heinemann.

Rosenblatt, Louise M. 1985. *The Reader, the Text, the Poem: The Transactional Theory of the Literary Work.* Carbondale: Southern Illinois University Press.

Scanlan, Christopher. 1996. *Best Newspaper Writing 1996.* Los Angeles: Bonus Books.

———. 1999. *Best Newspaper Writing 1999.* Los Angeles: Bonus Books.

Schanzer, Rosalyn. 2013. "Making History Books That Shine." *I.N.K. (Interesting Nonfiction for Kids)* (blog). February 5. http://inkrethink.blogspot.com/2013/02/making-history-books-that-shine_5.html.

Stewart, Melissa. 2012. "Behind the Books: The Creative Core." *Celebrate Science* (blog). September 19. http://celebratescience.blogspot.com/2012/09/behind-books-creative-core.html.

Strunk, William Jr., and E. B. White. 1999. *Elements of Style.* New York: Longman.

Vare, Robert. 2000. "The State of Narrative Nonfiction Writing." *Neiman Reports* Fall. www.nieman.harvard.edu/reportsitem.aspx?id=100535.

Wiki.answers.com. "How Do Seahorses Eat Their Food?" Available at http://wiki.answers.com/Q/How_Do_Seahorses_Eat_Their_Food%3F_Answer&action=view&isLookUp=1#Q=How%20Do%20Seahorses%20Eat%20Their%20Food%3F%20Answer.

Zinsser, William. 2006. *On Writing Well: The Classic Guide to Writing Nonfiction.* 30th anniversary ed. (7th ed., rev. and updated). New York: HarperCollins.

Opinion Books

Baylor, Byrd. 1995. *The Best Town in the World.* San Diego: Harcourt. (Grades 3–5)

Cherry, Lynne. 2000. *The Great Kapok Tree: A Tale of the Amazon Rain Forest.* Boston: Sandpiper/Houghton Mifflin Harcourt. (Grades K–3)

Layne, L. Steven. 2003. *My Brother Dan's Delicious.* Gretna, LA: Pelican. (Grades 2–5)

Teague, Mark. 2003. *Dear Mrs. La Rue: Letters from Obedience School.* New York: Scholastic. (Grades K–3)

Viorst, Judith. 1993. *Earrings!* New York: Atheneum Books for Young Readers. (Grades 1–3)

Science Texts

Aronson, Marc. 2012. *The Skull in the Rock: How a Scientist, a Boy, and Google Earth Opened a New Window on Human Origins.* Washington, DC: National Geographic Children's Books. (Grades 5+)

Aston, Dianna Hutts. 2007. *A Seed Is Sleepy.* San Francisco: Chronicle Books. (Grades 1–4)

Bishop, Nic. 2008. *Frogs.* New York: Scholastic Nonfiction. (Grades 1–4)

Butterworth, Chris. 2006. *Sea Horse: The Shyest Fish in the Sea.* Cambridge, MA: Candlewick. (Grades 1–3)

Cherry, Lynne. 2000. *The Great Kapok Tree: A Tale of the Amazon Rain Forest.* Boston: Sandpiper/Houghton Mifflin Harcourt. (Grades K–3)

Davies, Nicola. 1997. *Big Blue Whale.* Cambridge, MA: Candlewick. (Grades K–3)

———. 2001a. *Bat Loves the Night.* Cambridge, MA: Candlewick. (Grades K–4)

———. 2001b. *One Tiny Turtle.* Cambridge, MA: Candlewick. (Grades 1–4)

———. 2003. *Surprising Sharks.* Cambridge, MA: Candlewick. (Grades 1–4)

George, Jean Craighead. 1996. *One Day in the Desert.* New York: HarperCollins. (Grades 1–5)

Gibbons, Gail. 1990. *Beacons of Light: Lighthouses.* New York: Morrow Junior Books. (Grades 2–4)

Hatkoff, Juliana, Isabella Hatkoff, and Craig Hatkoff. 2011. *Winter's Tail: How One Little Dolphin Learned to Swim Again.* New York: Scholastic. (Grades 1–3)

Heard, Georgia. 1992. *Creatures of Earth, Sea, and Sky: Animal Poems.* Honesdale, PA: Boyds Mills. (Grades K–5)

Heinz, Brian J. 2005. *Butternut Hollow Pond.* Minneapolis: First Avenue Editions. (Grades 2–4)

Hirschmann, Kris. 2003. *Owls, Bats, Wolves and Other Nocturnal Animals.* New York: Scholastic. (Grades 3–5)

Hoose, Phillip M. 2012. *Moonbird: A Year on the Wind and the Great Survivor B95.* New York: Farrar Straus Giroux Books for Young Readers. (Grades 6+)

Jackson, Ellen. 2011. *The Mysterious Universe: Supernovae, Dark Energy and Black Holes.* Boston: Houghton Mifflin Harcourt. (Grades 5–7)

Lasky, Kathryn. 2003. *The Man Who Made Time Travel*. New York: Farrar, Straus, and Giroux. (Grades 4–6)

Lourie, Peter. 2009. *Whaling Season: A Year in the Life of an Artic Whale Scientist*. Boston: Houghton Mifflin Books for Children. (Grades 4–8)

———. 2012. *The Polar Bear Scientists*. Boston: Houghton Mifflin Books for Children. (Grades 4–8)

Malyan, Sue. 2005. *Bugs: A Close-Up Look at Insects and Their Relatives*. New York: DK. (Grades 2–5)

Markle, Sandra. 2011. *The Case of the Vanishing Golden Frogs: A Scientific Mystery*. Minneapolis: Milbrook. (Grades 4+)

Montgomery, Sy. 2001. *The Snake Scientist*. Boston: Houghton Mifflin Harcourt. (Grades 5–8)

———. 2009. *The Quest for the Tree Kangaroo: An Expedition to the Cloud Forest of New Guinea*. Boston: Houghton Mifflin Harcourt. (Grades 4–9)

———. 2010. *Kakapo Rescue: Saving the World's Strangest Parrot*. Boston: Houghton Mifflin Harcourt. (Grades 5–8)

Newquist, H. P. 2012. *The Book of Blood: From Legends and Leeches to Vampires and Veins*. Boston: Houghton Mifflin Harcourt. (Grades 5–8)

O'Connell, Caitlin. 2011. *The Elephant Scientist*. Boston: Houghton Mifflin Harcourt. (Grades 5–8)

Pledger, Maurice. 2008. *Sounds of the Wild: Ocean*. San Diego: Silver Dolphin Books. (Grades K–3)

Pringle, Lawrence. 2011. *Billions of Years, Amazing Changes: The Story of Evolution*. Honesdale, PA: Boyds Mills. (Grades 3+)

Rizzo, Johnna. 2010. *Oceans: Dolphins, Sharks, Penguins and More!* Washington, DC: National Geographic Children's Books. (Grades 4–6)

Ryan, Pam Muñoz. 2001. *Hello Ocean*. Watertown, MA: Charlesbridge. (Grades K–4)

Simon, Seymour. 1999. *Whales*. Boston: Houghton Mifflin Harcourt. (Grades 3–6)

Turner, Pamela S. 2009. *The Frog Scientist*. Boston: Houghton Mifflin Harcourt. (Grades 5–8)

Waring, Geoff. 2009. *Oscar and the Bat: A Book About Sound*. Cambridge, MA: Candlewick. (Grades K–3)

Webb, Sophie. 2011. *Far from Shore: Chronicles of an Open Ocean Voyage*. New York: Houghton Mifflin Books for Children. (Grades 3+)

Winter, Jeanette. 2011. *The Watcher: Jane Goodall's Life with the Chimps*. New York: Schwartz and Wade. (Grades K–3)

History and Social Studies Texts

Aronson, Marc. 2010. *If Stones Could Speak: Unlocking the Secrets of Stonehenge*. Washington, DC: National Geographic Children's Books. (Grades 5–8)

Borden, Louise. 2009. *A. Lincoln and Me*. New York: Scholastic. (Grades 1–3)

D'Aulaire, Ingri, and Edgar Parin D'Aulaire. 2008. *Abraham Lincoln*. San Luis Obispo, CA: Beautiful Feet Books. (Grades 3–6)

Evans, Shane W. 2011. *Underground: Finding the Light to Freedom*. New York: Roaring Brook. (Grades 1–3)

Fleming, Candace. 2011. *Amelia Lost: The Life and Disappearance of Amelia Earhart*. New York: Schwartz and Wade. (Grades 4–8)

Freedman, Russell. 1998. *Kids at Work: Lewis Hine and the Crusade Against Child Labor*. New York: Clarion Books. (Grades 5+)

———. 2007. *Who Was First? Discovering the Americas*. New York: Clarion Books. (Ages 9+)

Giblin, James Cross. 2004. *Secrets of the Sphinx*. New York: Scholastic. (Grades 6–12)

Hopkinson, Deborah. 2012. *Titanic: Voices from the Disaster*. New York: Scholastic. (Grades 5–8)

Kalman, Maira. 2012. *Looking at Lincoln*. New York: Penguin Group. (Grades K–3)

Lasky, Kathryn. 2003. *The Man Who Made Time Travel*. New York: Farrar, Straus, and Giroux. (Grades 4–6)

Levine, Ellen. 2007. *Henry's Freedom Box: A True Story from the Underground Railroad*. New York: Scholastic. (Grades K–3)

Michelson, Richard. 2008. *As Good as Anybody: Martin Luther King Jr. and Abraham Joshua Heschel's Amazing March Toward Freedom*. New York: Alfred A. Knopf. (Grades 1–4)

Nelson, Kadir. 2011. *Heart and Soul: The Story of America and African Americans*. New York: Balzer and Bray. (Grades 2+)

Partridge, Elizabeth. 2009. *Marching for Freedom: Walk Together, Children, and Don't You Grow Weary*. New York: Viking Juvenile. (Grades 6–12)

Rappaport, Doreen. 2009. *Eleanor, Quiet No More: The Life of Eleanor Roosevelt*. New York: Hyperion Books for Children. (Grades 3–8)

Ross, Stewart. 2011. *Into the Unknown: How Great Explorers Found Their Way by Land, Sea, and Air*. Cambridge, MA: Candlewick. (Grades 4+)

Ryan, Pam Muñoz. 1999. *Amelia and Eleanor Go for a Ride*. New York: Scholastic. (Grades K–3)

Shea, Pegi. 2009. *Noah Webster: Weaver of Words.* Honesdale, PA: Boyds Mills. (Grades 4–7)

Sheinkin, Steve. 2012. *Bomb: The Race to Build—and Steal—the World's Most Dangerous Weapon.* New York: Flash Point. (Grades 5+)

Stewart, Melissa. 2012. *Titanic.* Washington, DC: National Geographic Society. (Grades 1–4)

Tavares, Matt. 2012. *Henry Aaron's Dream.* Cambridge, MA: Candlewick. (Grades 3–5)

Tunnell, Michael O. 2010. *Candy Bomber: The Story of the Berlin Airlift's "Chocolate Pilot."* Watertown, MA: Charlesbridge. (Grades 4–6)

Wadsworth, Ginger. 2012. *First Girl Scout: The Life of Juliette Gordon.* Boston: Clarion Books. (Ages 9+)

Walker, Sally M. 2009. *Written in Bone: Buried Lives of Jamestown and Colonial Maryland.* Minneapolis: Carolrhoda Books. (Grades 6–9)

Weitzman, David. 2010. *Skywalkers: Mohawk Ironworkers Build the City.* New York: Flash Point. (Grades 6–10)

History and Science Narratives

Armstrong, Jennifer. 2006. *The American Story: 100 True Tales from American History.* New York: Knopf Books for Young Readers. (Grades 4–7)

Aronson, Marc. 2005. *Witch-Hunt: Mysteries of the Salem Witch Trial.* New York: Atheneum Books for Young Readers. (Grades 9+)

Aronson, Marc, and Marina Budhos. 2010. *Sugar Changed the World: A Story of Magic, Spice, Slavery, Freedom, and Science.* New York: Clarion Books. (Grades 8+)

Bartoletti, Susan Campbell. 2005. *Hitler Youth: Growing Up in Hitler's Shadow.* New York: Scholastic Nonfiction. (Grades 7–10)

Burns, Loree Griffin. 2010. *Tracking Trash: Flotsam, Jetsam, and the Science of Ocean Motion.* Boston: Houghton Mifflin Harcourt. (Grades 5–8)

Bruchac, Joseph. 1998. *A Boy Called Slow.* New York: Puffin. (Grades 3–6)

Cherry, Lynne. 2000. *The Great Kapok Tree: A Tale of the Amazon Rain Forest.* Boston: Houghton Mifflin Harcourt. (Grades K–3)

Cobb, Vicki. 2010. *What's the Big Idea? Amazing Science Questions for the Curious Kid.* New York: Skyhorse. (Grades 3–6)

Colman, Penny. 2002. *Where the Action Was: Women War Correspondents in World War II.* New York: Crown Books for Young Readers. (Grades 7+)

Deem, James. 2008. *Bodies from the Ice: Melting Glaciers and the Recovery of the Past.* Boston: Houghton Mifflin Harcourt. (Grades 5–8)

Delano, Marfe Ferguson. 2009. *Earth in the Hot Seat: Bulletins from a Warming World.* Washington, DC: National Geographic Children's Books. (Grades 4–6)

Freedman, Russell. 2007. *Who Was First? Discovering the Americas.* New York: Clarion Books. (Ages 9+)

George, Jean Craighead. 1997. *Everglades.* New York: HarperCollins. (Grades 2–5)

Giblin, James Cross. 2007. *The Many Rides of Paul Revere.* New York: Scholastic. (Grades 3+)

Hakim, Joy. 2004. *The Story of Science: Aristotle Leads the Way.* Washington, DC: Smithsonian Books. (Grades 5–8)

Harness, Cheryl. 2008. *The Ground-Breaking, Chance-Taking Life of George Washington Carver and Science and Invention in America.* Washington, DC: National Geographic Children's Books. (Grades 4–8)

Hatkoff, Isabella, and Craig Hatkoff. 2006. *Owen and Mzee: The True Story of a Remarkable Friendship.* New York: Scholastic. (Grades 1–5)

Heiligman, Deborah. 2011. *Charles and Emma: The Darwins' Leap of Faith.* New York: Square Fish. (Grades 8+)

Hoose, Phillip. 2010. *Claudette Colvin: Twice Toward Justice.* New York: Square Fish. (Grades 6+)

Jackson, Donna M. 2002. *The Wildlife Detectives: How Forensic Scientists Fight Crimes Against Nature.* Boston: Houghton Mifflin Harcourt. (Grades 4–7)

Jackson, Ellen. 2011. *Mysterious Universe: Supernovae, Dark Energy and Black Holes.* Boston: Houghton Mifflin Harcourt. (Grades 5–7)

Murphy, Jim. 2003. *An American Plague: The True and Terrifying Story of the Yellow Fever Epidemic of 1793.* New York: Clarion Books. (Grades 6–10)

Nelson, Kadir. 2008. *We Are the Ship: The Story of Negro League Baseball.* New York: Hyperion Books. (Grades 3+)

Partridge, Elizabeth. 2009. *Marching for Freedom: Walk Together, Children, and Don't You Grow Weary.* New York: Viking Juvenile. (Grades 6–12)

Sís, Peter. 2007. *The Wall: Growing Up Behind the Iron Curtain.* New York: Farrar, Straus, and Giroux. (Grades 3+)

Stone, Tanya Lee. 2009. *Almost Astronauts: Thirteen Women Who Dared to Dream.* Cambridge, MA: Candlewick. (Grades 5–7)

Thimmesh, Catherine. 2006. *Team Moon: How 400,000 People Landed Apollo 11 on the Moon.* Boston: Houghton Mifflin Harcourt. (Grades 5+)

Walker, Sally M. 2009. *Written in Bone: Buried Lives of Jamestown and Colonial Maryland.* Minneapolis: Carolrhoda Books. (Grades 6–9)

Weatherford, Carole Boston. 2006. *Moses: When Harriet Tubman Led Her People to Freedom.* New York: Hyperion Books for Children. (Grades 2–5)

Biographies

Bass, Hester. 2009. *The Secret World of Walter Anderson.* Cambridge, MA: Candlewick. (Grades 2–6)

Byrd, Robert. 2012. *Electric Ben: The Amazing Life and Times of Benjamin Franklin.* New York: Dial. (Grades 4–6)

Freedman, Russell. 2012. *Abraham Lincoln and Frederick Douglass: The Story Behind an America Friendship.* New York: Clarion Books. (Grades 4+)

Krull, Kathleen. 2009. *The Boy Who Invented TV: The Story of Philo Farnsworth.* New York: Knopf Books for Young Readers. (Grades 2–5)

Nivola, Claire A. 2012. *Life in the Ocean: The Story of Oceanographer Sylvia Earle.* New York: Farrar, Straus, and Giroux. (Grades K–3)

Rappaport, Doreen. 2012. *Helen's Big World: The Life of Helen Keller.* New York: Hyperion Books for Children. (Grades K–4)

Schubert, Leda. 2012. *Monsieur Marceau: Actor Without Words.* New York: Flash Point. (Grades K–3)

Shea, Pegi. 2009. *Noah Webster: Weaver of Words.* Honesdale, PA: Boyds Mills. (Grades 4–7)

Stone, Tanya Lee. 2013. *Who Says Women Can't Be Doctors? The Story of Elizabeth Blackwell.* New York: Henry Holt. (Grades K–3)

Wadsworth, Ginger. 2012. *First Girl Scout: The Life of Juliette Gordon.* Boston: Clarion Books. (Ages 8+)

Books on Teaching Nonfiction Writing

Caine, Karen. 2008. *Writing to Persuade: Minilessons to Help Students Plan, Draft, and Revise, Grades 3–8.* Portsmouth, NH: Heinemann.

Dorfman, Lynne R., and Rose Cappelli. 2009. *Nonfiction Mentor Texts: Teaching Informational Writing Through Children's Literature, K–8.* Portland, ME: Stenhouse.

Fletcher, Ralph, and JoAnn Portalupi. 2001. *Nonfiction Craft Lessons: Teaching Information Writing K–8.* Portland, ME: Stenhouse.

nfiction Matters: Reading, Writing, and Research in
: Stenhouse.

. 2010. *Writing to Explore: Discovering Adventure*
3–8. Portland, ME: Stenhouse.
ction Writing: A Practical Guide. New York:

. Hoyt. 2012. *Explorations in Nonfiction Writing.* Portsmouth,
..and/Heinemann.

Nonfiction Websites & Blogs

animals.nationalgeographic.com
DOGOnews: Fodder for Young Minds
I.N.K. (Interesting Nonfiction for Kids). http://inkrethink.blogspot.com/
Teach Mentor Texts. www.teachmentortexts.com/
kids.discovery.com
Meetmeatthecorner.org
A Year of Reading: Two Teachers Who Read. A Lot. http://readingyear.blogspot.com/
Wonderpolis.org

Prizes for Nonfiction Children's Books

AAAS/Subaru SB and F Prize for Excellence in Science Books. www.sbfonline
.com/Subaru/Pages/CurrentWinners.aspx
The Cybils Awards. www.cybils.com/
Green Earth Book Awards. www.natgen.org/
NCTE Orbis Pictus Award for Understanding Nonfiction for Children. www.ncte
.org/awards/orbispictus
Robert F. Sibert Informational Book Medal. www.ala.org/alsc/awardsgrants/
bookmedia/sibertmedal